ELEANOR ROOSEVELT'S LIFE OF SOUL SEARCHING AND SELF DISCOVERY

*From Depression and Betrayal
to First Lady of the World*

Ann Atkins

Flash History Press

ELEANOR ROOSEVELT'S LIFE OF SOUL SEARCHING AND SELF DISCOVERY
From Depression and Betrayal to First Lady of the World

By Ann Atkins

Published by: Flash History Press LLC
Address: P.O. Box 184
 Paoli, PA 19301
Website: www.AnnAtkins.com

ISBN: 978-0-9834784-0-9
Library of Congress Control Number: 2011928255
First Edition. Printed in the United States of America
10 9 8 7 6 5 4 3 2 1

Photos from Franklin D. Roosevelt, Presidential Library and Museum

Page Design by One-on-One Book Production, West Hills, California

Cover Design by Lindsey Mottola with Argus Printing and Invitation Studio, Wayne, Pennsylvania

Technical support by Amy Kate Amer

Author Photo by Dave Campli – Campli Photography, Malvern, Pennsylvania

DEDICATION

to
Edward J. Atkins, Colonel, USAF (retired)
My husband, my friend—thank you
for your gift of love,
endless support and
the thesaurus.
Your dedication to excellence is my standard.

ACKNOWLEDGMENTS

The art of writing expands past the singular experience at the keyboard. Keeping a vibrant flow of creativity is possible because of the rejuvenating love from those around me.

Cory,
Blaine,
Amanda,
the beauty of your lives, your brave and bold spirits—
it is my honor to be your mother

Thank you—Aunt Birdie, who for all my life has been
"The Listener"

Thank you—Colleen for giving me the book,
Women Who Run With the Wolves

Thank you—Amy Kate—your creative ideas and
technical support—priceless

Victoria, Josee, Riley, Dawn, Asi and Lynn—my pack
of fierce women who will not let me settle for less

Thank you—to those who took the time to read
and critique the evolving manuscript:
Pat, Ed, Birdie, Nick, Mom, Colleen,
Vicki, Riley and Emily

TABLE OF CONTENTS

PART ONE
A BITTER BEGINNING

Flash
Context and Comments - - - - - - - - - - 3

Chapter One
Childhood - - - - - - - - - - - - 5

Chapter Two
Adolescence - - - - - - - - - - - 13

Chapter Three
Marriage- - - - - - - - - - - - 20

Chapter Four
Crisis - - - - - - - - - - - - 31

Reflections for the Reader - - - - - - - - 36

PART TWO
AWAKENING

Flash
Context and Comments - - - - - - - - - - 41

Chapter Five
Emancipation - - - - - - - - - - - 44

Chapter Six
Compassion - - - - - - - - - - - 50

Chapter Seven
Causes - - - - - - - - - - - - 64

Chapter Eight
War - - - - - - - - - - - - - 87

Reflections for the Reader - - - - - - - - 94

PART THREE
POLITICAL, PUBLIC AND PERSONAL STORMS

Flash
Context and Comments   -   -   -   -   -   -   -   -   99

Chapter Nine
Critics   -   -   -   -   -   -   -   -   -   -   103

Chapter Ten
Refuge   -   -   -   -   -   -   -   -   -   -   108

Chapter Eleven
Blindsided By Family   -   -   -   -   -   -   -   117

Reflections for the Reader   -   -   -   -   -   -   122

PART FOUR
LIFE AFTER DEATH

Flash
Context and Comments   -   -   -   -   -   -   -   -   125

Chapter Twelve
Pragmatic Plans For Peace   -   -   -   -   -   -   128

Chapter Thirteen
United Nations – An Oxymoron   -   -   -   -   -   134

Chapter Fourteen
Elanor   -   -   -   -   -   -   -   -   -   -   144

Reflections for the Reader   -   -   -   -   -   -   151

Bibliography   -   -   -   -   -   -   -   -   153

Endnotes   -   -   -   -   -   -   -   -   155

Index   -   -   -   -   -   -   -   -   -   166

PART ONE
A BITTER BEGINNING

FLASH

Context and Comments

Knowing the context of Eleanor's era deepens the value of her accomplishments.

Through the span of Eleanor's life, from 1884 - 1962, the laws of science make quantum leaps forward. She will read newspaper headlines of an aircraft flying a few hundred feet, to jets breaking the sound barrier and man going to outer space. It's the end of boiling water on a wood stove and the beginning of popcorn in the microwave. And the science of war excels as the details of strapping a gas mask on a war horse is exchanged for a diagram of strapping an atomic bomb on an airplane.

"Liberty and justice for all," is far from being realized.

The veterans of the North and South gather at Gettysburg for the 50 Year Reunion of the Civil War. At this time it is much easier to plan if the 'Negroes' are not invited.

Women won't be given the right to vote until 1920, which is a glaring irony considering Queen Victoria has been capable of ruling the whole British Empire from 1837-1901—64 years.

For the young, their lives read like gruesome chapters in a Charles Dickens novel. Two million children provide cheap labor in coal mines, canneries and steel mills. There are no laws protecting children, but there are laws to protect animals.[1] In the late 1800s the first recorded successful case to protect an abused child is won by declaring the child as part of the animal kingdom. It will not be until 1938 when a minimum age and work hours are federally regulated.

Are these the "the good old days" if life expectancy is a brief forty-five years? Millions die each year of infectious diseases and thirty-five thousand die every year in industrial accidents. There is no workers' compensation, no unemployment pay and no insurance. Severance pay is given because something at work got severed—a hand or a foot.

In any arena Eleanor fights injustice and perseveres against overwhelming odds and chilling cruelties. Like Wonder Woman in support hose, she will win battles on the local, the national and the global scale. Her life is an example of moral courage and she becomes internationally known as "First Lady of the World."

First, she must survive her childhood.

1
CHILDHOOD

B aby Eleanor is born into the ostentatious display of upper class opulence known as the "Gilded Age."

Eleanor's mother, Anna Livingston Ludlow Hall, is the belle of the ball for New York City. Basking in self-assurance, she can thumb her nose at guest lists that include the Vanderbilts and Astors. Anna also knows that within her lineage is a signer of the Declaration of Independence. This gives her self-esteem a dash of superiority. Now she just needs a husband.

Eleanor's future father, Elliott Roosevelt, has a checkered past that would land anyone else in a jail cell, rehab or the morgue. Elliott's excuses include sibling rivalry with his overachieving brother, the future President Theodore Roosevelt. Avoiding his brother's shadow, Elliott enjoys adventurous hunting trips in India, China and Ceylon. Health problems are exacerbated in a struggle with sexual identity, alcohol and shame. His misery is exposed in his letters to home.[2]

In 1881, Elliott returns from his latest trip. He is in New York City and meets Anna. Having these two characters in place, the stage is set for a tragic play of which Shakespeare would be proud.

With all the passion and commitment of a charming alcoholic, Elliott writes about Anna, "a Sweet Hearted, a true, loving Earnest Woman.... Womanly in all purity, holiness and beauty, an angel in tolerance, in forgiveness and in faith..." [sic][3] This list reflects Elliott's romantic ideals, not Anna's character. Anna, equally unrealistic, is flattered with the attention of the most eligible bachelor in New York City.

Like media coverage of movie stars, Anna and Elliott's daily affairs are frequently featured in the newspapers. Anna marries Elliott and this couple has the smug security of knowing they 'belong.'

Eleanor is born, and Anna is disappointed that her first born child is not a boy. Adding to this frustration, Anna describes her daughter as, "a more wrinkled and less attractive baby than the average."[4] As Eleanor grows, it is obvious that her character is as somber as her physical appearance is plain.

Eleanor's habit of waiting quietly in the doorway, waiting and wanting to be acknowledged, and waiting to be asked in have been deemed 'shy.' Anna intensifies Eleanor's insecurities by belittling her. Eleanor remembers her mother saying to any company in the room, "She's such a funny child, so old-fashioned, that we always

Eleanor, Long Island, New York, 1887

call her 'Granny.'" Eleanor says of those times, "I wanted to sink through the floor in shame …" [5]

"I would sit at the head of her bed and stroke her head. The feeling that I was useful was perhaps the greatest joy I had experienced." Eleanor's childhood memory of being with her mother. [6]

It will be at least twenty five years until Eleanor learns to boldly walk in or walk out of any door she wants. But now a child, she is starving for attention and acceptance. One light in her life is her father. Here she is needed.

Elliott has not been successful in any of the lucrative jobs that are put in place for him. His life is a constant cycle of mishaps from foolish accidents, drugs, drinking, hostile episodes at home, and then, absence away from the family. When Elliott returns, he can withstand Anna's harsh rebukes only by going to Eleanor for unquestioning acceptance. In exchange for this adulation, Elliott dotes on his 'dear little Nell.' Eleanor glories in the attention and it gives her some feeling of worth.

Eleanor Roosevelt and her father Elliott in New York City

Anna has a second child and is pleased to have produced a son, but the good news doesn't halt the gradual disintegration between her and Elliott. In an effort to stop the downward spiral, Anna decides to pack up the family and tour Europe. Any happy moments are distorted with the dread that Elliott will start drinking or is already drunk.

The visit to Paris coincides with Anna's due date for a third child. Eleanor is shunted off to a convent to live until after the baby is born. Eleanor is not even six.

Alone in a foreign country, Eleanor feels cast aside by her family and could use some reassurance from the nuns. Seeing another little girl comforted because she swallowed a coin, Eleanor tells the nuns she too has swallowed a coin. The nuns are suspicious and discover Eleanor has lied.

Anna, disgraced by Eleanor's actions, comes to retrieve her daughter. Eleanor recalls, "I remember the drive home as one of utter misery, for I could bear swift punishment far better than long scoldings."[7]

The strain of keeping the family intact is taking a toll on Anna. Elliot threatens suicide and is now living with a mistress in Paris. When his estate is signed over to Anna, he promises to get better. Not convinced, Anna packs up the children and heads back to New York. The worst of it, what is most unforgiveable, is the family shame is made public. The headlines in the New York *Herald* declare:

ELLIOTT ROOSEVELT DEMENTED BY EXCESSES.

WRECKED BY LIQUOR AND FOLLY, HE IS NOW CONFINED IN AN ASYLUM FOR THE INSANE NEAR PARIS

PROCEEDINGS TO SAVE THE ESTATE

COMMISSIONERS IN LUNACY APPOINTED ON PETITION OF HIS BROTHER THEODORE AND HIS SISTER ANNA WITH HIS WIFE'S APPROVAL[8]

When Elliott finally returns to New York City he plays for Eleanor's sympathy. When Anna learns that Elliott has an illegitimate child and that the mother is making a ploy to go public, she limits the contact he has with his children.

Eleanor and her father keep in touch by writing. During her growing years of seven to nine, Eleanor spends her days waiting for another letter. The arrivals are sporadic, but the empty promises that unfold from each envelop are constant. Elliott stokes the delusion that some day he will return, and they will live happily together.

Anna, as the sole guardian for the children, is busy ensuring their future. In the event anything should happen to her, Grandmother Hall, Anna's mother, will have custody of Eleanor and her two brothers. In fact, Anna and the children move back to live with Anna's mother. Extra bedrooms are not the problem, since Grandmother has two mansions, one on the Hudson River for the summer and one in New York City for the winter.

Tragic stories of Anna and Elliott continue. The family has so deteriorated that when Anna is dying of diphtheria, she refuses to let Elliott come to see her. Within months of this loss, Eleanor's brother Ellie dies of scarlet fever. Eleanor remembers, "Death meant nothing to me, and one fact wiped out everything else—my father was back and I would see him very soon."[9]

Elliott's brief visits to Eleanor and her brother Hall show that the ravages of this man's self-absorption have warped any vestiges of kindness and doting. Elliot's need to still appear cavalier is indulged when taking Eleanor on reckless horse cart rides. During these brash jaunts, Eleanor tries desperately to win his approval and not show her fear.[10] When he comes by to take her for a walk with the dogs, Eleanor swallows any anger and disappointment as Elliott uses this opportunity to stop by his club and have a drink. Eleanor is left waiting. On one occasion she stands for six hours while holding the dogs. She sees her father carried out and it's the doorman who takes Eleanor back to Grandmother Hall's house.

Clinging to dreams of a home with her father, Eleanor is in denial of these disappointing episodes. Her indomitable spirit will someday win accolades from around the world, but right now it is pitifully misdirected.

Elliott continues to send endearing letters to Eleanor, but there won't be many more. His brother Teddy writes, "Elliott is up and about again: and I hear is drinking heavily; if so he must break down soon."[11] Two days after Teddy's declaration, this prediction will come true.

Elliott has been using 'stimulants' again, suffering from delusions, and at some point, jumps out a parlor window. He is knocked unconscious and dies. A newspaper article covering the story politely recalls the past. "There was a time when there were not many more popular young persons in society than Mr. and Mrs. Elliott Roosevelt."[12]

Members from Elliott's side of the family want Eleanor to be sent to Allenswood, an all girl school in England. Family aunts had attended this school and Eleanor's parents had previously met and been impressed with the head teacher. The idea is rejected by Grandmother Hall who claims she wants the grandchildren home to keep a close eye on them.

Grandmother Hall, a prior debutante herself, is only fifty-one and has her own problems. The trouble started when her husband passed away several years ago. Mr. Hall had always controlled the money and the children. While lavish parties and Parisian clothes for his family kept up public appearances, the private reality was a strict code of conduct for exuberant children.

When he dies, the monastic ambiance goes with him. Mrs. Hall, treated as a child herself, is ill-equipped to run the house full of their children. At the time of Eleanor's stay their ages range from 16-25. With behaviors reflecting varying levels of self-indulgence, romantic flings and drinking, the mood of the mansion has ramped up to the raucous level of a frat house. To support these excesses, Mrs. Hall is using the trust funds of her grandchildren.

"Playing with children was difficult for me because play had not been an important part of my own childhood. Eleanor reflecting back on her childhood."[14]

Eleanor and her younger brother Hall have a yearly income of $7,500[13] which equates to approximately $180,000 per year in today's money. This wealth is not reflected in Eleanor's wardrobe. She has two dresses. If one gets dirty in play, and the other hasn't been washed yet, she must wear a dirty dress. Adding to this misfit appearance is her height. For years her dresses are short, shapeless and outdated because they are remade hand-me-downs from the aunts.

This goes from bad to worse.

Friends for Eleanor are few and far between. They are afraid to come and visit. The uncles, too often intoxicated, have been known to start shooting a gun out of the second story window over the heads of approaching guests.

On top of that, there is Madeleine. She's the governess who could easily be mistaken as Cinderella's step mother.

How cruel is it when someone who has been pulling your hair now cuts holes in the socks that you just darned? Madeleine compounds the torment by bestowing kindness to Eleanor's brother Hall. Eleanor's cousin recalls, "I remember Madeleine. She was a terrifying character. It was the grimmest childhood I have ever known. Who did she (Eleanor) have? Nobody."[15]

Grandmother does provide more structure to her granddaughter's daily life. On occasion, Eleanor's uncles teach her how to play tennis, ride a bike and jump with her pony. With her aunts, Eleanor recites poetry, enjoys music and goes rowing on the Hudson River. Eleanor's education, which prior to this has been sketchy, is now filled in with literature, French, German and piano lessons.

These could be degrees of improvements for Eleanor's life, but if sporadic afternoons of attention are compensation for outbursts from drunk uncles and drama queen aunts then the balance toward a healthy environment is in the red.

Often alone, Eleanor spends time escaping to a dream world in her books and grows even more remote. Eleanor's cousin remembers the house, "I never wanted to go. The grim atmosphere of that house. There was no place to play games, unbroken gloom everywhere. We ate our suppers in silence. The general attitude was, 'don't do this.'"[16]

2

ADOLESCENCE

As the aunts become young women, they have commandeered the library to smoke cigarettes and carouse with their male visitors. The uncles escalate their escapades to such an extent that Grandma is now worried about Eleanor's safety. A friend of Eleanor's asked why there are three locks on the inside of her bedroom door. Eleanor answers, "To keep my uncles out."[1]

Grandmother Hall decides it is time to send Eleanor away to school.

The year is 1899. The emphasis of education for women is preparation for future dinner parties not politics or public policy. Luckily, the teachings at Allenswood contradict these conventions. The students, all female, are expected to expand their mental horizons, and become independent thinkers with their own commitment to personal and social responsibility. It is perfect for Eleanor.

Within the first year, Eleanor earns respect and regard as one of the girls' primary 'go to' resources. Fellow students needing advice, a compassionate shoulder to lean on or help with their studies, recognize Eleanor's kindness and willingness to assist. Eleanor's heart of compassion is acknowledged. No one calls her 'Granny.'

Eleanor is becoming confident and her personality is flourishing. She is picked for the field hockey team and she remembers back to that day as "One of the proudest moments of my life."[2]

"It was once said that men did not marry women who showed too much intelligence. In my youth I knew women who hid their college degrees as if they were one of the seven deadly sins. But all that is passing and so will pass many other prejudices that have their origin in the ancient tradition that women are a by-product of creation."[3]

In classes and discussions, Eleanor is expected to give thoughtful commentary not a parroted 'politically correct' response. She is encouraged to hammer out her own logic and assert her own opinions. Eleanor's intense and serious perspective is appreciated by Mlle. Souvestre, the head teacher.

Taking a personal interest in Eleanor, Mlle. Souvestre gives her motherly attention in grooming and health. Encouraged to shop for herself, Eleanor enjoys clothes that are up to date and appropriately fit her elegant six-foot figure. Future critics who decry her as a drudge should be reminded that one of her first choices for a new dress is a glamorous deep red fabric—hardly the color for a stick-in-the-mud.

Mlle. Souvestre keeps Grandmother Hall informed about Eleanor. Mlle. Souvestre writes, "All that you said when she came here of the purity of her heart, the nobleness of her thought has been verified by her conduct among people who were at first perfect strangers to her... I often found that she influenced others in the right direction. She is full of sympathy for all those who live with her and shows an intelligent interest in everything she comes in contact with. As a pupil she is very satisfactory, but even that is of small account when you compare it with the perfect quality of her soul."[4]

Holidays are spent going to London theater and visits to Paris. Mlle. Souvestre requests Eleanor accompany her on a summer trip to Italy. Eleanor, now sixteen, is thrilled with the opportunity to be in charge of tickets, train schedules, and packing the trunks. She experiences local foods, wines and traipsing around Florence by herself. It's a far cry from the lonely child shutting herself away in her bedroom to read books.

Eleanor Roosevelt, school portrait, 1898

Eleanor has to go home for the following summer, and her Aunt Pussie arrives in London to escort her back to New York. Pussie, one of Grandmother Hall's daughters, is accustomed to Eleanor being a sympathetic listener to the details of her latest romantic crisis. Now Pussie finds that Eleanor has become accustomed to responding with her own opinion and having that opinion valued. This is not what Aunt Pussie wants.

Pussie's revenge is telling Eleanor that because of her looks, she will never find a man to be interested in her. Pussie then unleashes the ultimate ammunition: all the scandalous stories about Elliott. Eleanor is crushed.

Eleanor goes to her grandmother to have this information disputed. Instead, Grandmother confirms the stories and increases the anguish by telling Eleanor there is no one to escort her back to England at the end of the summer. Since social customs dictate that young ladies outside their homes must always be accompanied, Eleanor cannot go back to Allenswood.

Is Eleanor still the little girl that stands meekly in a doorway waiting for someone to tell her what to do? Will she fall into the rut of the rich and accept her shallow lot in life? If so, Eleanor will be nothing more than an obscure name on a branch of the Roosevelt family tree.

This may be Eleanor's first act of defiance. Eleanor finds a temporary nanny to escort her across the Atlantic, back to Allenswood.

At the end of the following school year, Grandmother insists it is time to come back to New York City for the start of the fall social season. Eleanor will be turning eighteen. It is time to find a husband.

Mlle. Souvestre sends Eleanor off with this letter, "From this very minute, when I am writing to you, life, your life, which is entirely new and entirely different, and in several respects entirely contradictory, is going to take you and drag you into its turmoil. Protect yourself to some extents against it, my dear child, protect yourself above all from the stand point of your health… Give some of your energy, but not all, to worldly pleasures which are going to beckon you. And even when success comes, as I am sure it will, bear in mind that there are more quiet and enviable joys than to be among the most sought after women at a ball… … A thousand and a thousand tendernesses to my Totty (Eleanor) whom I shall always love."[5]

It is the last time Eleanor will see her beloved teacher. They will correspond for the next few years and Eleanor will always have her photo nearby, but Mlle. Souvestre will die before Eleanor is able to visit England again.

Eleanor now resides at Grandmother Hall's New York City mansion. This might sound grand until you factor in Aunt Pussie is also living there and is more popular and histrionic than ever. Grandmother Hall stays up at the house on the Hudson still trying to cover for her alcoholic sons, although she lets Uncle Vallie come visit the city once in awhile for weekend binges. Eleanor, younger by several years, is expected to keep her aunt and uncle out of too much trouble.

During this first year back, Hall, Eleanor's only surviving younger brother, is away at a private school. It is Eleanor who writes him every day and visits him on holidays. Her sense of responsibility dictates that she takes on a mothering role for him and provide him a home. This additional duty is an emotional demand she juggles throughout Hall's life. Sadly, she will see this smart young man live a short life riddled with the poor decisions of an alcoholic.

The social season is starting and Eleanor is expected to gaily attend balls and cotillions as part of her 'coming out.' Akin to the marketing of toys at Christmas, the question to be answered is—*Who* will be the belle of the ball? This is determined by who can create the biggest 'buzz' i.e. attract the most dance partners, the most glamorous dresses, the most articles in the social column, and be the most beautiful. All this effects the rest of a woman's life since this is her *only* legacy.

Eleanor's mother had been the belle of the ball. Eleanor's aunts, each year of their own coming out had also been the belle of the ball, her Grandmother Hall had been the belle of her ball. Eleanor was not. She writes of that time, "I knew I was the first girl in my mother's family who was not a belle and, though I never acknowledged it to any of them at that time, I was deeply ashamed."[6]

Because Eleanor's Uncle Teddy is the President of the United States, the newspaper social columns are careful to not call his niece's debut a failure, otherwise she might have suffered more humiliation. Instead articles about Eleanor are filled in with nostalgic memories of her mother's beauty and charm.

Did Eleanor read these columns and realize she had missed the mark? Did the other debutantes turn their heads to whisper cruel comments behind her back? Eleanor acknowledges, "…I was struggling through in formal society each night, and yet I would not have wanted at that age to be left out, for I was still haunted by my upbringing and believed that what was known as New York Society was really important."[7]

In this Siren's call of the Gilded Age, Eleanor tries to follow her heart and do meaningful work for the poor. She volunteers at a settlement house in the city.

The settlement movement is a social reform effort of the late 1800s to have the rich and the poor live more closely together—diversify the neighborhood. The focus is a 'settlement house' in a poor urban area that houses middle-class volunteers who can help provide food, academic instruction and cultural lessons to the low income neighbors, particularly children.

Eleanor has done charity work before but from a distance. She has visited hospitals and orphanages with her family during holidays to help with such niceties like decorating a Christmas tree. Now she dives in to her new "volunteer world." Refusing rides with her friends in carriages, she chooses public transportation and starts learning a new point of view. Eleanor writes, "The dirty streets, crowded with foreign-looking people, filled me with terror, and I often waited on a corner for a car, watching, with a great deal of trepidation..."[8]

In the midst of volunteering and the debutante balls, Eleanor is seeing Franklin. One afternoon he comes with her to parts of New York City he has never known. He is stunned by the living conditions of these people.

Eleanor is touched by this soft spot in Franklin's heart, and she opens up to him. She starts becoming needier of his presence in her daily life and begins conceding her goals at the settlement house for his political dreams.

Mlle. Souvestre's letter "...your life, which is entirely new and entirely different, and in several respects entirely contradictory, is going to take you and drag you into its turmoil...." is about to become a fulfilled prophecy.

3

MARRIAGE

~

Franklin, aside from being Eleanor's fifth cousin once removed, is an only child. For every moment of callous neglect in Eleanor's life, Franklin was being pampered and coddled by two parents. At eight years old he writes, "Mama left this morning and I am going to take my bath alone."[1] 'Mama' is Sara Delano Roosevelt.

Able to recite her Delano lineage back to William the Conqueror, Sara can trump anyone who dares to compare their family history with hers. This haughty heritage is her greatest gift to Franklin. She declares, "My son Franklin is a Delano, not a Roosevelt at all."[2] Sara conveniently ignores that her family's wealth came from the lucrative but unseemly business trade of opium.

Sara lives and breathes Society, which at that time was so important it really did have a capital 'S.' Enjoying her position at the peak of this pyramid, Sara cannot imagine having Jews or politicians in her beloved mansion any more than she can imagine someday having a mixed-race president.

Stories prevail in polite whispers about Sara's intrusive interactions into the minutest detail of Franklin's life. A family friend says of her, "She was an indulgent mother but would not let her son call his soul his own."[3] Franklin's father isn't much better.

James Roosevelt, a widower, is fifty-two when he marries Sara who is twenty-six. They reside at Springwood, their estate on the Hudson River. James is every bit as committed to

Franklin Delano Roosevelt and his mother, Sara Delano Roosevelt, 1887

raising Franklin as is Sara. He teaches Franklin to swim, fish, ride, hunt, sail and golf. James envisions that his son will carry on the country squire position which he is carefully crafting. With the airs of an English nobleman, James can outsnob the Vanderbilts who live up the road. When an invitation comes from them for dinner, James refuses on the grounds, "If we accept we will have to have these people in our home."[4]

James' saving grace from this imperious perspective is his teaching Franklin a recurring motif of the Roosevelt families— to ease the suffering of the lower class. Sara isn't so impressed with this trait, but James manages to pass it on to Franklin.

This ability for Franklin to reach past his own egocentric behaviors and consider the plight of the less fortunate is the point of connection he shares with Eleanor. It is this spark during their courtship that will keep them together during tumultuous years ahead.

Franklin is attending Harvard when his father dies. Because Sara can't bear to be alone she rents a house in Boston to be near her son. During this time, Franklin has started seeing Eleanor. Whether it is devious or self preservation, Franklin has not told his mother about Eleanor and his plans to marry her.

When Sara is informed about her son's intentions, she is not pleased. She extracts from Franklin the promise that he will keep the engagement a secret for one year. The year includes tickets for a six week cruise to the Caribbean. There are three first class reservations; one for Sara, one for Franklin and one for any friend of his as long as it isn't Eleanor. Franklin agrees.

"If you would just run a comb through your hair, dear, you'd look so much nicer." Sara speaking to Eleanor[5]

Eleanor's desire to appease degrades her standard of integrity when she accepts Franklin's agreement to keep the engagement secret. Living a falsehood is not Eleanor's forte. Although she follows the rules of decorum and does not express her emotions directly, it makes her angry. If she does lash out, she immediately follows with an apology. She writes to Franklin, "I've come to the conclusion that I need someone to watch over my temper, it makes me so cross with myself to lose it, and yet, I am forever doing it."[6]

Frustrated with Sara's iron will to interfere, Eleanor's own iron will emerges to win Sara over. Practiced in the craft of placating, Eleanor knows the first thing to do is look small and exude helplessness. Eleanor does this with both Sara and Franklin. She has been signing her letters to Franklin just as she had her father; 'Your dear little Nell.'

Eleanor's ability to diminish her desires becomes apparent as her work at the settlement house starts taking a back burner. Wanting to see Franklin more often she writes him, "I would not be going I'm afraid, but one must do something, or not having the person who is all the world to me would be unbearable."[7]

Sara talking to Eleanor, Campobello, 1904

Eleanor has hardly considered her volunteering a mere 'something.' In fact, her personal commitment has annoyed relatives, and they worry she will bring home some disease. Now that she is reverting back to being politely involved, she cuts herself off not only from the work she loves but from female friends who support her independence. Eleanor, nineteen years old, could join a couple of these ladies and go to college. She doesn't. She continues to shift her interests to Franklin.

Franklin talking to Eleanor, Campobello, 1904

"It was a wife's duty to be interested in whatever interested her husband, whether it was politics, books, or a particular dish for dinner." Eleanor explaining the social realities of her time.

For anyone shaking their head in wonder and asking, "Why is she doing this?" It is a valid question.

The few years of nurturing support Eleanor received at Allenswood have not been enough to counterbalance the effects of her dysfunctional family and this tightly scripted society. In a letter to Franklin, Eleanor writes, "I feel lost without you somewhere near. I used to think myself so self-sufficient, but I'm learning too quickly how much of my happiness lies in someone else's hands...."[8]

What about Franklin? For a man whose insulated life and nonchalance has earned him the nickname 'Feather Duster,' Eleanor, with her serious demeanor, hardly seems a fit. There are other debutantes eager to accommodate Franklin's frivolous ego.

What Eleanor gives is a younger version of what Franklin's mother started. Franklin is to be the center of her attention. But there is more. Eleanor also provides a means to meet his professional aspirations.

The history of what motivates Franklin is thoroughly documented in various biographies. They all concur that Franklin loves power, and he is looking to politics to best fulfill this ambition. Considering the deluge of stories that proclaim Franklin's abilities to successfully scheme—is it a mere coincidence that he chooses Eleanor whose uncle is the president?

The couple survives the year of secrecy imposed by Sara, and eventually their engagement is announced. Notes of congratulation follow. It is one of the few times Franklin is not the lead attraction. A secretary of Franklin's later writes, "... he said that when his engagement was announced, all the congratulations were showered on him for securing Eleanor as a wife. He felt, he said, that some people, at least, should have congratulated her for securing him as a husband."[9]

Not everyone will agree with Franklin. An old school mate of Eleanor's is not at all impressed with the match. She makes note that Franklin is "by no means good enough for her."[10]

Sara maintains the opposite. She has gone along with her son's wishes, but the undercurrent remains; Eleanor is not welcome. Sara's wedding gift to Eleanor is a choker necklace. The style is also known as a 'dog collar.'

Eleanor wants Uncle Teddy to give her away. March 17 is available if the wedding can be arranged around the president attending the St. Patrick's Day Parade in New York City. Eleanor and Franklin are married March 17, 1905.

Their honeymoon in Europe is a yo-yo of emotional intimacy and distance. After a few wonderful days in Venice, they travel north, and Franklin suggests a hike up the mountains. Eleanor demurs, and Franklin trots off with another American woman who has been flirting with him. They are gone till after dark.

Eleanor wearing her wedding dress, 1905

Eleanor doesn't see that she is back in the same position as with her father. Her hopes and feelings are carelessly tossed aside, and she is waiting again. Instead, Eleanor berates herself and says, "I never said a word. I was jealous beyond description."[11] This will lead to years of passive aggressive behaviors in Eleanor as Franklin will be a womanizer the rest of his life.

In England, Eleanor continues building a doormat persona. While they are visiting friends, Eleanor is asked to give a talk to open the local fair. Her initial reaction is, "quite certain that I could never utter a word aloud in a public place."[12]

On the trip home Eleanor thinks she is suffering from sea sickness. It's morning sickness.

Back in New York City, Sara has insisted she will make housing arrangements for the newlyweds. She has also gone ahead and completely furnished the place and staffed it with servants of her choice. It is conveniently three blocks from Sara's city house.

Sara's disregard for her daughter-in-law's preferences successfully muzzles Eleanor's opinions in anything. Franklin, never wanting to confront his mother, doesn't ever come to Eleanor's defense. A tag team for wrestling would marvel at this match up. Sara's subversive attacks, and Franklin's ability to exploit Eleanor's fears is constantly keeping Eleanor off balance. Eleanor reflects back on this time and says, "Instead of taking an interest in these houses, one of which I was to live in, I left everything to my mother-in-law and my husband."[13]

True to the rules of polite society, Eleanor does not ever reveal the honest version in public statements about her personal life. It is left for us to wonder how she felt when Sara visited and presumed to rearrange the furniture. What leverage is Eleanor left with when this Grandma buys horses for her grandsons after Eleanor had taken away their ponies as punishment? Any hint of the truth Eleanor covers with excuses or takes the blame herself. She maintains this stance to the grave.

"I looked at everything from the point of view of what I ought to do, rarely from the standpoint of what I wanted to do. There were times when I almost forgot that there was such a thing as wanting anything." She writes in he autobiography.[14]

Franklin wants a big family, and so Eleanor has 6 children within the first 11 years of their marriage. She suffers the loss of the third child who dies at 8 months old. The roles of wife and mother take precedence over her own needs and any hope of confidence in these roles is extinguished with the constant overriding opinions of her mother-in-law.

Sara makes sure the children know they can always come to her for money and they will hear, "Your mother only bore you. I am more your mother than your mother is."[15] The son Elliott will later recall, "…Granny spoiled us and we could do no wrong in her eyes."[16] Eleanor comments about that time, "I was not allowed to take care of the children, nor had I any sense of how to do it."[17]

Eleanor and Franklin—During happy days at Campobello, 1910

Appeasing Sara, overbearing nannies and spending days living up to society's standards all lead to a painful and lonely distance between Eleanor and her children. She is unable to see the similar pattern of her own childhood where her emotional needs were neither acknowledged nor met.

Franklin is appointed Assistant Secretary of the Navy, and they move to Washington D.C. Eleanor dutifully performs the job of a Washington wife spending every afternoon out "calling" on the political wives in the city. Never staying more than six minutes, she sometimes makes ten to thirty visits a day. At one point, Eleanor is getting 2,000 invitations a year for Navy teas.[19]

> *I stand back and look at myself and think that isn't you as an individual, that is you as the personage you may happen to have to be for this period of time.*
> Eleanor's "My Day" column[18]

Eleanor is expected to keep up the social entertaining at home too. During one dinner party at their house Eleanor goes upstairs to say good night to the children. She delays going back downstairs for so long that Franklin comes to find her. She tells him, "I just can't stand to greet all those people. I know they all think I am dull and unattractive. I just want to hide up here."[20] Eleanor is 29 years old.

At a fund raising luncheon with hundreds of ladies, Eleanor is asked to speak. She wants to say 'no,' but Sara is in the audience. Eleanor gets up and makes a request for donations which results in several thousand of dollars being raised. In spite of this she says, "I trembled so, that I did not know whether I could stand up, and I am quite sure my voice could not be heard."[21]

Eleanor and Franklin are fitting neatly into the prescribed pattern for Washington D.C. couples. Franklin is free to pursue his dreams, and Eleanor acquiesces to the job of supporting him. Eleanor acknowledges she has become "a completely colorless echo of my husband and mother-in-law and torn between them. I might have stayed a weak character forever if I had not found that out." [22]

So the questions begging to be asked are: "How does she finally find out she's being a 'weak character'?" and "How much longer is this going to continue?"

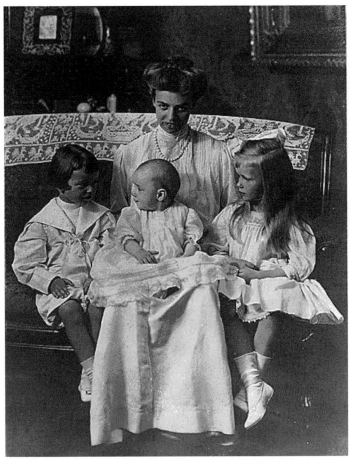

Eleanor Roosevelt with children, James, Elliott and Anna in Hyde Park, 1911

Eleanor is getting to the point of finally pushing back. She writes, "The bottom dropped out of my own particular world, and I faced myself, my surrounding, my world honestly for the first time. I really grew up that year."[23]

4

CRISIS

It's the summer of 1918; Eleanor will be turning thirty-four. She and Franklin are still in Washington D.C. World War I will finish in a few months with an international casualty count that exceeds 37 million.

Over the years, Eleanor has struggled to exceed the expectations for a political wife and mother of five children. Her reputation has grown along with her skills at being organized and running a house. She is "the good wife," and

Eleanor Roosevelt, 1915

Sunday evenings at the Roosevelt residence has become the

place to be. At these events Eleanor enjoys lively political conversation and policy debate. Her ability to translate for foreign visitors from France or Germany is quaintly juxtaposed to her serving their traditional Sunday evening meal—scramble eggs.

A benefit to the war (WWI), if there can be one, is the social restrictions being relaxed and wives are not expected to be out calling every afternoon. With that obligation deferred, Eleanor is free to do more meaningful work. At the Red Cross motor corps Eleanor learns to drive. She sets up the Red Cross canteen and with other women organizes the Navy Red Cross. She gives comfort and company to troops coming in and out of Washington, which includes making coffee, handing out sandwiches and knitting wool socks.[1]

To help her with the multitude of duties is Lucy Mercer, Eleanor's social secretary. For the last four years, Lucy has become Eleanor's friend and a fill-in nanny for the Roosevelt children; Anna 12, James 11, Elliot 8, Franklin 4 and John 2.

"I guess one of the sad things in life is that rarely do a man and woman fall equally in love with each other and even more rarely do they so live their lives that they continue to be lovers at times and still develop and enjoy the constant companionship of married life." Summer 1943, reflecting on the emotional distance between her and Franklin[2]

During the summers the family packs up and goes to Campobello, Franklin's family home in Maine. This yearly tradition started when Franklin was a child because his father had always encouraged a love of the outdoors, swimming in the ocean and sailing. Franklin has wanted to pass this on to his own children.

For Franklin to break from this plan is troubling for Eleanor. The last couple years, 1917 and 1918, Franklin has begged off from going with the excuse of work.

His insistence that Eleanor should still go to Campobello alone and take the children has her worried.

Eleanor has conceded to Franklin's nights out, men's clubs, stag parties and flirtations as long as they are just that, flirtations. Her distrust to leave Franklin alone in D.C. is veiled by voicing minor worries. Franklin writes this letter of reassurance to her, "I really can't stand that house all alone without you, and you were a goosy girl to think or even pretend to think that I don't want you here *all* the summer, because you know I do! But honestly *you* ought to have six weeks straight at Campo, just as I ought to, only you can and I can't! I know what a whole summer here does to people's nerves and at the end of this summer I will be like a bear with a sore head … as you know I am unreasonable and touchy now—but I shall try to improve."[3]

His sincere professions are a smoke screen. In September, Eleanor discovers a packet of letters written to Franklin. Eleanor's world shatters. The feminine handwriting and words of endearment are not hers. Franklin has betrayed her trust. And it is Lucy who has betrayed Eleanor's friendship.

The depth of the deception goes deeper as Eleanor comes to understand that Washington society is in cahoots with Franklin's philandering. Eleanor's cousin, Alice (President Roosevelt's daughter), who has always been jealous of her father's attention to Eleanor, has taken particular pleasure in having Lucy and Franklin over for parties when Eleanor is out of town.

"And, having learned to stare down fear, I long ago reached the point where there is no living person whom I fear, and few challenges that I am not willing to face."[4] Autobiographical writings when 75 years old

Eleanor tells Franklin he can have a divorce. Franklin weighs his options.

If Franklin goes through with a divorce, his mother is threatening to turn off the money, putting an abrupt end to his life of private clubs and yachting. Lack of funds, divorce and remarrying Lucy, a Catholic, will also end his political career.

Franklin promises Eleanor he will never see Lucy again. Franklin saves face with Lucy using the excuse that Eleanor won't give him a divorce.

A final weight in Eleanor's emotional sorrow is the double standard she must live by—Franklin's affair is not publicly exposed. In 1918 it is inconceivable that the jilted woman will reveal her husband's affair and expect any public support. She will have pity, but the tide of public opinion will be sympathetic with the man.

Eleanor leaves indirect hints to 'talk' about the affair and its effect on her. This poem, *"Psyche"* by Virginia Moore is one of the clues:

> *The soul that has believed*
> *And is deceived*
> *Thinks nothing for a while*
> *All thoughts are vile.*
> *And then because the sun*
> *Is mute persuasion,*
> *And hope in Spring and Fall*
> *Most natural,*
> *The soul grows calm and mild,*
> *A little child,*
> *Finding the pull of breath*
> *Better than death…*
> *The soul that had believed*

And was deceived
Ends by believing more
Than ever before.

It was found in the nightstand of Eleanor's bedroom after her death. At the top of the paper Eleanor had inscribed, "1918."

Reflections for the Reader

"There are only two or three human stories, and they keep on repeating themselves as fiercely as if they had never happened before."

Willa Cather, O Pioneers!

Part One — Bitter Beginnings

The struggle of surviving bad parenting is a classic story line. Look at Walt Disney movies like *Cinderella*. The step mother's ego has unrealistic expectations for her daughters. Cinderella suffers under the berating bitterness of this delusion.

Eleanor bears the burden of her mother's and her father's delusions.

A measure of how deep the childhood emotional scars go does not correlate to the degree of a trauma. It correlates to how the adults in power handle pressure and have honest expectations.

In the movie *Star Wars* Luke has Obi Wan Kenobi. In the movie *Rocky*, it's the boxing coach.

Eleanor has her teacher, Mademoiselle Souvestre.

Survivors who succeed have at least one person who believed in them.

In the 'hero's journey' the excitement is often when the hero is getting out of trouble that their naiveté and emotional needs got them into i.e. *Pinocchio*.

Eleanor, with her insecurities, makes her share of mistakes.

The overwhelming evidence is this: Eleanor learned from

her experiences and moved on.

When Eleanor and Franklin married they were both young and immature. Wow! That's got to be a first!

For some couples they can grow and stay together. For others they grow and separate. For others they stagnate so as not to upset the status quo.

In the movie *Romancing the Stone*, Joan Wilder and Jack Colton have plunged over a waterfall. This is the crisis. Jack, not seeing Joan thinks she has died. When she pops up Jack calls out to her, "I thought you drowned." Joan replies, "I did." Joan continues her story, now as a stronger woman.

Eleanor's 'plunge' was for months not seconds and there was no Prince Charming waiting for her. She was alone.

A crisis can be seen as a challenge to let the old self die.

PART TWO
AWAKENING

FLASH

Context and Comments

September of 1918 coincides with a bestselling book. It's the talk of the town in Washington D.C. To appreciate the dark irony this plays out for Eleanor, here is a quick historical digression.

At the start of the American Revolution, John Adams is a Boston lawyer and argues the defense of the British soldiers involved in the Boston Massacre. Not exactly a career making choice, but John stands for justice even when it favors the enemy. He reminds the courtroom, "Facts are stubborn things, and whatever may be our wishes, our inclinations, or the dictates of our passion, they cannot alter the state of facts and evidence."

John wins the case, and it doesn't appear to be a detriment to the family name. He becomes a Founding Father, the second president of the United States and his son, John Quincy Adams, becomes the sixth president.

The first part of John's quote, *"Facts are stubborn things,"* has remained popular to this day.

Henry Adams (1838-1918), John Quincy's grandson, knows his great grandfather's famous words too. He also knows that facts like his having an affair and his wife's consequential suicide, will tarnish his image. So rather than argue the facts Henry simply withholds the facts.

Here are the facts

Clover (1843-1885) is an early pioneer in photography, is part of the 'in crowd' in Washington society and is a linguist whose work helps her husband's research in writing a book for which he will become famous. Much like Eleanor's selfless devotion to Franklin, Clover abides by her husband's wishes to not pursue photography as anything more than a hobby. When offers are made to purchase her photos, she demurs to Henry's demand to say 'no.'

Clover discovers her allegiance does not buy her husband's fidelity. Her anguish is doubled upon knowing the affair is with a younger woman who has been a long time family friend to both Clover and Henry. Clover kills herself with the chemicals she used to create her photos. She swallows potassium cyanide.

Henry tosses the red herring of 'depression' as the excuse for Clover's death and his 'grief' as the reason for him destroying all evidence of Clover's existence.

In a grave with no name, Clover is buried at Rock Creek Cemetery outside of Washington D.C. Henry commissions a bronze statue as a memorial. This cloaked seated figure is created with shoulders slumped back to the granite wall behind it. With the right hand in a listless touch to the cheek, the spiritless face, shrouded by a hood, stares vacantly at space in front of the knees. It is referred to as the *Grief* statue.

[To this day, a Google search of Henry Adams reports that his wife, Clover Adams, committed suicide because of depression. A Google search of Clover, repeats the same story. Henry's affair is omitted.]

Henry's book is published, *The Education of Henry Adams.* Readers wonder if it is possible that remorse wins over when they see that Henry wrote, "The American woman of the nineteenth century will live only as the man saw her … This is pure loss to history, for the American woman of the nineteenth century was much better company than the American man."[1] But alas, it is just another gross layer of guile and a means of buttering up to his paramour. She was reading and editing the initial manuscripts.

His book is a best seller and the buzz of Washington. Stories of Clover's demise resurface not in light of reading about her in Henry's autobiography but instead by Henry's omission. He has left out not only her suicide but any mention of their thirteen year marriage. Enjoying a dose of morbid humor, readers howl when in spite of the blatant omission in writing about his life, the book wins a Pulitzer Prize.

The year Henry's book is the talk of the town? The year a renewed remembrance of Clover's suicide is whispered over the rim of tea cups?

It is 1918 and this same crowd is buzzing because they also know that Lucy Mercer just got fired.

5

EMANCIPATION

Clover's memorial becomes Eleanor's refuge. Day after day, at Rock Creek Cemetery, Eleanor sits. She is unable to move on with life. Stuck in what she dreaded most, she is living a repeat tragedy of her mother and father. Her game of giving—didn't work.

As Eleanor spirals down this internal journey, so often called 'The Dark Night of the Soul,' does she seethe with self-loathing knowing she has complied with the rules of discretion and not made a public fuss? Henry Adams had dined at their house. Did she ever confront him? Does she choke on a sob recognizing her part in betraying Clover? Does she wonder if Franklin will follow the example of Henry if she should choose suicide? Will her existence be glossed over?

With the twisted expectations, do Eleanor's shoulders sag from the pressure in this culture to conform to the image of 'Good Wife' even if it kills you? Should she let it kill her too?

The headlines about Clover's death had read "Depression" and public opinions bolstered the rumors of Clover being unstable, pointing to other women in her family who suffered bouts of melancholy. This pat response is much more palatable. It is easier to acknowledge rather than upset the balance of power. In truth, Clover had been in a family of strong intelligent women. So was Clover's 'depression' really 'despair'?

Does Eleanor weep as she recognizes that society will stoop to the excuse of mental illness?

Remember always that you not only have the right to be an individual, you have an obligation to be one. A favorite saying of Eleanor's later in life.

During the months ahead, Franklin's efforts to be more thoughtful are minimal at best. At family gatherings he over indulges with drinking, is loud and obnoxious and still plays the ladies man. This is particularly embarrassing to Eleanor since she and her family remember the drunken episodes of her father.

Any solace from her children is wishful thinking. Outmaneuvered by Sara's money and the spoils of living at Springwood, Eleanor is pigeonholed in the role of being a disciplinarian. This script is further amplified when the children are shielded from the truth and do not understand their mother's mental anguish. They only see that their mother is cross and unhappy.

Eleanor says of those days, "There are times in everyone's life when the wish to be done with burdens and even of this life seems, overwhelming."[2]

After weeks of dark pondering Eleanor gradually realizes another option. She will stop living by the dictates of others and start living her life her own way, the Eleanor way. She will say many times in the years ahead, "Life is meant to be lived. That's all there is to it."[3]

Franklin, Sara, Eleanor and children, Campobello, 1920

Her transformation is not overnight. Sara will challenge the change. And Franklin is still going to be…Franklin.

Three years after the affair, there is a second major event that is to alter Eleanor's life. Franklin is diagnosed with infantile paralysis, Polio. He is paralyzed from the waist down. Without the aid of leg braces, he will never walk again.

Eleanor is a constant nurse and companion.

Adding to the strain of caring for her husband and meeting the needs of their children is the war of wills with her mother-in-law. Sara wants her son to retreat from public life and come back to Springwood.

Is Eleanor tempted to side with Sara? She would not only

win her mother-in-law's favor but also the keys of control over Franklin.

However, Eleanor supports Franklin's decision to press on with any rehabilitation possibilities and then return to politics. This confrontation with Sara is an early sign that Eleanor is standing up for what she wants for her family. Eleanor also knows she doesn't want to be tied to the job of being Franklin's gate keeper. She will help keep Franklin's political dreams alive while he convalesces and she is pursuing her own interests.

"I think I am pretty much of a fatalist. You have to accept whatever comes and the only important thing is that you meet it with courage and with the best that you have to give." On Edward R. Murrow's radio program "This I Believe"

Years later when Eleanor reflects back to this time she comments that it "… made me stand on my own two feet in regard to my husband's life, my own life and my children's training."[4]

Eleanor gets involved with the International Congress of Working Women. These women, famous activists in their own right, help educate her about underlying social injustices. Eleanor also joins and gives speeches for groups such as the League of Women Voters and the Women's Trade Union League. She petitions for playgrounds, public housing, school lunches, nursing facilities, unemployment insurance and workers compensation. She writes articles for magazines like *Redbook* and *McCall's* and teaches classes while being vice principal at Todhunter, a school for girls.

Do one thing every day that scares you. A favorite saying of Eleanor's.

In 1926, Eleanor is picketing with three hundred other women in support of a group on strike. She makes headlines, not for picketing, but for being arrested. She and seven other women "of prominence" are taken in for ignoring police orders to move on and "disorderly conduct."[5]

Unknown, Nancy Cook, Eleanor Roosevelt, Marian Dickerman in Campobello, 1926

Striding toward authenticity is not a straight line forward for Eleanor. Societal constraints are such that women aren't supposed to acknowledge they enjoy a good political fight any more than they can acknowledge they like sex. Eleanor's reports back to Franklin are wrapped in wording that also allays her lingering needs to assure her place at Franklin's side as his supportive secondary. She writes, "You need not be proud of me dear, I'm only being active till you can be again—it isn't such a great desire on my part to serve the world, and I'll fall back into habits of sloth quite easily."[6]

Eleanor's choice of self-deprecation is interesting. She is pointing out, by means of derision, her greatest asset. Far from ever having 'habits of sloth,' this woman is a barrel of industrial-strength energy. Her critics, the media, and her friends all acknowledge it is exhausting to keep up with her. Aside from a grueling schedule, she knits. She knits while waiting to give a speech, during meetings, or giving dictation. She is always knitting. It is Franklin who cries out in mock despair, "Lord, just let Eleanor be tired."[7]

Building a new life takes time, and there are long days when Eleanor is still struggling. A lonely sigh can be heard as her pen scratches in her journal the day of her birthday, "I am 35. Margaret and Hall sent me a book. Mama and Tissie and Franklin wired."[8] Everyone is busy with their own life. Eleanor is alone.

The difference is this Eleanor will do something about her loneliness. **The old Eleanor would have stood at the door, waiting.**

Eleanor Roosevelt, shooting pistol at Chazy Lake, New York, 1934

6

COMPASSION

~

Franklin has spent seven years convalescing. Eleanor's support, along with Franklin's political team, leads to Franklin becoming governor of New York in 1928.

Eleanor, happy for Franklin's success, does not let his new position overshadow her personal goals and ambitions. She keeps her own schedule and earns her own money. She does not revert back to being, "a completely colorless echo."

Part of Eleanor's 'color' is she now recognizes her joy in giving as an essential part of her being. Both personally and publicly her compassion reaches out to fill hearts and homes that are struggling. Living up to her intention to ignore the gossip and dictates of society, she champions for the rights of African Americans, Jews, women and children. Building alliances and friendships, she enjoys the company of women who are feminists and activists, many in long standing lesbian relationships.

With the Democratic Convention (1932) and the possibility of Franklin becoming president, Eleanor dreads the thought of losing this life she has made for herself. If she is to become the First Lady to the United States, Eleanor knows the public scrutiny of her independent life, her friends, and being outspoken for unpopular causes will be brutal. She is terrified and writes in a letter to a friend that she "Could not live in the White House."[1]

But it doesn't matter. In November, Franklin wins the election. Eleanor is asked if her life will now "belong to the public after this." Eleanor replies, "It never has and never could."[2]

When asked to visit the White House prior to moving in, Eleanor turns down the offer for the White House car and military aid to pick her up. Her plans are to arrive by train the night before, and in the morning, walk to the White House. In spite of this, the chief of protocol for the State Department shows up at the hotel with the limousine. Eleanor sticks to her guns. She and her friend walk to the White House.

The friend, Lorena Hickock, fondly known to Eleanor as 'Hick' is an Associated Press reporter who was assigned to cover Eleanor during the presidential campaign. Hick's devotion and friendship is a source of strength and a shoulder to lean on through the years ahead as they escape the intrusive glare of D.C. with getaway weekends and hikes in Yosemite Park.

For the inauguration, Franklin has it in mind for everyone to go by train. Eleanor announces she "would load her roadster with belongings and drive down with a woman friend [Hick]."[3] Franklin insists Eleanor go with his entourage. Eleanor relents.

In the morning hours before the inauguration, Eleanor takes Hick to Rock Creek Cemetery. Wanting to share with a friend a part of her painful past, they sit at the statue of *Grief.* Eleanor may be back in D.C. again, but she is not the same woman and she is not alone.

> *Friendship with oneself is all-important, because without it one cannot be friends with anyone else in the world. Eleanor Roosevelt*

As First Lady, Eleanor learns how to stay true to herself and to the people who need her help. For the hundreds of invitations she receives she realizes, "It is really the position which is invited and not the person."[4] She knows that officials do not want to meet her, Eleanor, but the "wife of the President."[5]

Eleanor is enjoying setting new standards and challenging overprotective rules. When Amelia Earhart comes to town in her airplane, Eleanor goes up for a ride at night. The *New York Times* reports, "The First Lady of the Land and the first woman to fly the [Atlantic Ocean] went skylarking together tonight in a big Condor plane."[6] Eleanor thinks nothing of dismissing police sent to guard her at public events or dismissing the elevator usher at the White House. When she opens the door for the elevator she is told by the usher that the elevator is run only by doormen and not by her. Eleanor gets in the elevator by herself. While closing the door she gives him this reply, "Now it is." [7]

In the first twelve months at the White House, she receives over 300,000 pieces of mail. At one engagement she shakes hands with 3,100 people in 1 1/2 hours.[8]

Her demeanor is a far cry from her earlier years when she ran upstairs to hide from a few guests. In the first year as First Lady, 1933, this is the record of people with whom she meets:

For meals	4,729
Overnight guests	323
Tea Guests	9,211
Received	14,056
Total	28,319

Several hundred more can be added to this number since, aside from this, she travels and gives 45 paid lectures that year.

Eleanor's Support Team—Malvina Thompson and Edith Helm, Washington D.C. 1941

It's understood she is not the one that cooked the meals, changed the bed sheets or shopped for groceries. Instead, she maintains her gracious manners as she shakes thousands of hands, greets people warmly, carries on conversation, and indulgently overlooks boorish guests vying to impress her. Changing sheets would be an easy day.

Her early awkwardness and insecurities vanish, to the point where she can say, "Four hundred will be quite easy to have for tea."[9] And to keep up with this pace Eleanor does suggest that "After every 500 guests take a sip of water."

With the official duties under control, Eleanor is learning to use the leverage that her position provides. She is constantly reminding the public about the plight of people around them. She uses her "My Day" newspaper column to broaden the horizons of her readers and help open their eyes to the suffering of others. In today's terms this would be comparable to Michelle Obama having a daily blog. Imagine Eleanor with a Facebook page.

Once unable to stand and make a public appeal for money, she now shows no qualms about making an audience gasp at the New York Metropolitan Opera. Between Act 1 and 2, Eleanor gets up and walks onto center stage. She faces the audience to make a request for money on behalf of those struck by the Depression. She explains to the audience, "When you come face to face with people in need, you simply have to try to do something about it."[10]

Eleanor also becomes savvier when dealing with the media. She has the inside help of her friend Hick. Eleanor not only conducts her own press conferences, she flaunts the 'men only' rule at press conferences with Franklin, making hers only for women journalists. Since newspapers want to carry stories about Eleanor, this policy gives job assurance for many female reporters. What critics deem conniving, Eleanor sees as leveling the playing field.

Her press conferences make great stories for the journalists because Eleanor will bring up controversial topics. She tells them, "Sometimes I say things which I thoroughly understand are likely to cause unfavorable comment in some quarters, and perhaps you newspaper women think I should keep them off the record. What you don't understand is that perhaps I am making these statements on purpose to arouse controversy and thereby get the topics talked about and so get people to thinking about them."[12]

> "My grandmother had taught me that a woman's place was not in the public eye, and that idea had clung to me all through the Washington year."[11] (When Franklin was Assist. Sec. to the Navy).

Eleanor's ability to combat head games is not what wins over the hearts of people. It is abundant compassion that warms thousands of lives. Like sunshine on the vineyards of Napa Valley, the following examples represent only a few of the 'grapes.'

Compassion on a Personal Level

Eleanor arranges for a fourteen year old girl, Bertha, to receive medical care. Bertha is in the hospital for ten months. During that time, Eleanor sends flowers, gifts and notes. Eleanor keeps in touch with Bertha, signs her diploma[13], helps her get a job, finds Bertha's brother a job, attends Bertha's wedding and is a godmother to her child.[14]

Eleanor finds out the police have chased away the peanut vendor that has always stationed his cart near the White House. Although sick in bed, she writes a note to have this matter resolved, "I would myself miss him on that corner. We had better let him stand at the White House again." [16]

> "Whatever comes your way is yours to handle."[15] Eleanor Roosevelt

During her stay as First Lady, Eleanor says, "My feeling about the White House is that it belongs to the people. Their taxes support it. It is theirs. And, as far as possible, they should be made to feel welcome here."[17] During her 13 years in residence she has hundreds of overnight guests. In 1936 she asks a couple dozen women from the Women's Trade Union League to stay at the White House. It is the first time working women have been White House guests.[18] As a thoughtful gesture, Eleanor makes sure a New York City dressmaker is given the Lincoln bedroom. The woman exclaims, "Imagine me, Feigele Shapiro sleeping in Lincoln's bed!"[19]

For the years of suffering during the Depression, there are plenty of opportunities to help people. One time when Eleanor stops at a gas station, a man approaches her and asks for money. She asks him why he doesn't go to the Civilian Conservation Corps (CCC) that provides jobs. He tells her they don't accept people without a home address. Eleanor gives him her card with her New York City address and $10. She invites him to dinner the following Monday. The man, Al Kresse, shows up. Eleanor puts in a call to the CCC and then informs Al he can start work tomorrow. She asks Al if he has a place to sleep tonight. Al says 'no' and Eleanor lets him stay at her apartment. Al does well at the CCC and keeps in touch with Eleanor. She has Al and his parents to the White House for dinner, they correspond for years and Eleanor becomes the godmother to his daughter.[20]

Do what you feel in your heart to be right—for you'll be criticized anyway. You'll be damned if you do, and damned if you don't. Eleanor Roosevelt

In April 1936, as First Lady, she is the chair for the Washington Committee on Housing and the Southern Democrats are outraged. Eleanor has invited Negroes. During her speech Eleanor's empathy of the race issues so moves an African American woman that she "had to retire in tears because she was so touched by the understanding and sympathy for her race that was expressed by Mrs. Roosevelt's manner as well as her speech."[21]

Soup Kitchen for the unemployed, 1936

In 1939, Eleanor writes about traveling by train through Tennessee. She relays a scene out her window, not as a sterile reporter giving hollow facts but with insight to a child's world. "I saw a little girl, slim and bent over, carrying two heavy pails of water across a field to an unpainted house. How far that water had to be carried, I do not know, but it is one thing to carry water on a camping trip for fun during a summer's holiday, and it is another thing to carry it day in and day out as a part of the routine of living."[22]

And her compassion and work ethics don't end as she gets older.

When she is in her seventies and could be slowing down, she says she will do a television commercial for margarine. She is disregarding the unwritten code to be dignified and traditional. She figures with the money she earns ($35,000) she can save 6,000 lives with CARE packages.[23]

And this last example is classic Eleanor.

At seventy-five she is a world renowned stateswoman. She is in New York City on her way to a charity meeting to give a speech. As she is leaving her hairdresser, an African American youth backs his car into her and knocks her down. This being 1959 Eleanor doesn't want to chance a racial incident and tells the young man to hurry on before people can gather. She wants to keep her schedule of speaking at the charity but first her doctor tapes up her torn ligaments. She goes to the engagement at the Waldorf-Astoria and apologizes to her audience for having to make her speech while sitting on a pillow. Eleanor says to her doctor later, "People saw that I was in pain, and we raised more money."[24]

Eleanor is often admonished for doing too much for people. She responds, "whatever comes your way is yours to handle." And "I do not attempt to judge others by my standards."[25]

In her book, *You Learn By Living*[26] she writes:

"Charitable organizations and hospitals, poverty and pain—these exist, alas, everywhere. Their needs are enormous, beyond calculation. But there are others, less dramatic though no less real. There is loneliness within reach of your outstretched arm; there is unhappiness that requires, perhaps, only understanding and a fortifying word; there is hunger and sickness and despair somewhere in your neighborhood."

Compassion on a Nationwide Level

Eleanor is adamant that compassion does not mean handouts. She says, "I get panicky every now and then about these people having work."[27] She wants it understood "charity may be necessary, [however] our aim should be to get people back to a point where they can look after themselves. I have never felt that people should be grateful for charity. They should rightfully be resentful and so should we look at the circumstances which make charity a necessity."[28]

Children of a rehabilitation clinic in Arkansas

By the 1930s the extent of the Great Depression on hard working Americans exposes that the American façade of rugged individualism is cracking apart. Society has become so entwined with a complex economy that its collapse has more serious consequences than in earlier years. Eleanor sees this and says, "We have believed in the individualistic thing. We can't go on that way. We must work together on big things."[29]

Civilian Conservation Corp, California, 1933

Providing Social Security is one of the 'big things.' Her commitment for this financial support to family life is evident when she explains low income families had, "done what good citizens should do and they simply had never been able to save. There had always been someone in the family who needed help; some young person to start…"[30]

When she receives bad press for wanting federal money spent on social programs Eleanor counters with "We spend a great deal of money every year" to improve "various crops and fruits and vegetables... It seems to me that the time has arrived when a certain amount of money should be spent on an experimental station for improving social conditions."[31]

MORE SECURITY FOR THE AMERICAN FAMILY

THE WIDOW OF A QUALIFIED WORKER WILL RECEIVE MONTHLY BENEFITS AT AGE 65. IN CERTAIN CASES, AN AGED DEPENDENT PARENT MAY GET BENEFITS. ...

FOR INFORMATION WRITE OR CALL AT THE NEAREST FIELD OFFICE OF THE
SOCIAL SECURITY BOARD

Social Security Poster

As of 1925, $200 million is spent annually for industrial and government research for companies like American Telegraph and Telephone, G.E. and DuPont. This and other New Deal jobs such as construction traditionally go to white men. Eleanor argues, "There is something fundamentally wrong with a civilization which tolerates conditions such as many of our people are facing today. We talk of a 'new deal' and we believe in it. But we will have no 'new deal' unless some of us are willing to sit down and think this situation out. It may require some drastic changes in our rather settled ideas, and we must not be afraid of them."[32]

One idea Eleanor promotes is to support the arts as a means of providing more jobs for minorities. She says, "I hope we will be able to look upon art and artists as one of the factors which can be used to draw nations together. ... We need emotional outlets in this country, and the more artistic people develop the better it will be for us as a nation."[33] The Federal Theatre Project (during the Depression) employs 5,644 people.[34] The Federal Music Program in 1937 employs 16,000 musicians. This includes 163 symphony and concert orchestras, 51 bands, 15 chamber music ensemble, 69 dance orchestras and 146 teacher projects.

Another prospect Eleanor takes a particular interest in is building the town of Arthurdale, West Virginia. This is the first of several planned New Deal resettlement towns designed to take impoverished laborers and move them to newly constructed rural communities helping them become economically self-sufficient. The first lady is so enthusiastic about the idea that she brings it to the attention of Franklin, who decides to federalize the project.

Eleanor makes monthly visits to Arthurdale. She personally reviews the plans for the houses being built. She listens to and knows the individual concerns of the families. She hands out diplomas at graduation. When there aren't enough funds to pay the teachers, Eleanor gives from her own money.

Measures of success for New Deal programs can be difficult to assess. Turning despair into aspirations doesn't directly show up on economic charts especially if politics and deprivation of federal funds deter the economic stability of jobs. The local citizens also have their own resistance to change. The Arthurdale community vote to make their town 'whites only.'

In 1994, at the 60-year-celebration of Arthurdale, the citizens had moved from being unemployed coal mining families to a generation of teachers, doctors, lawyers, artists, and military men and women.[35] To commemorate the anniversary, residents wore sweatshirts with the words:

Arthurdale
The Dream Lives On

7
CAUSES

Eleanor is relentless in her efforts to break any social conventions that are based on the subjugation of others. During her lifetime; children are tied to benches laboring through fourteen hour days, women working in a locked factory room will burn to death in a fire, Jews who have escaped genocide are denied entrance to American shores, and on display in a barber shop window, is the memento of the latest lynching—nigger knuckles in a jar.[1] What now smacks as atrocious, were justified practices, sacred cows of American society.

It is no surprising coincidence that people who benefit from these prejudices are among Eleanor's critics. She says of those who disapprove, "I suppose when one is being forced to realize that an unwelcome change is coming, one must blame it on someone or something."[2]

She also reminds us, "You can't move so fast that you try to change the mores faster than people can accept it. That doesn't mean you do nothing, but it means that you do the things that need to be done according to priority."[3]

Eleanor's array of causes for which she championed has filled books. This chapter highlights her advocacy for three groups; African Americans, women and Jews.

African Americans

Our Civil War, which put an end to slavery and an end to 970,227 lives, was a cataclysmic turning point for our nation. During Eleanor's lifetime the wounded from this war can be seen hobbling down the streets, Abe Lincoln's son is still alive, and children hear from grandmothers wistful ante-bellum stories about their good life and their good slaves. Eleanor's paternal grandmother was one of them, and Eleanor has her own prejudices to work through.

During the first move to D.C. in 1913, Eleanor, 29, has brought with the family the white servants. This doesn't comply with southern tradition so she replaces them with African Americans. Eleanor writes in a letter "Well, all my servants are gone, and all the darkies are here and heaven knows how it will turn out!"[4] Years later Eleanor corrects herself. She writes an apology for her poor choice of words in her autobiography, "I am terribly sorry if the use of the word "darky" offends …"[5]

The social climate for the early 1900s includes increased riots and lynchings against African Americans. Two dominant reasons are: 1.) The economy; white and black veterans coming back from WWI have no jobs. 2.) The society; African American troops are treated as equals by white Europeans and come back to the United States expecting the same.

During the summer of 1919 there are the Washington race riots. Eleanor, having taken the children to Campobello for the summer, writes to Franklin, "No word from you, and I am getting very anxious on account of the riots. Do be careful not to be hit by stray bullets."[6] Eleanor makes no mention of compassion for the African American cause or the victims in the riots. It is ten months after the Mercer affair, and she is still worried whether or not Franklin is faithful.

Eleanor's growth through the 1920s prepares her to now be an advocate for African Americans when Franklin becomes president. Having a dinner for the National Council of Women she includes future long time friend, Mary Jane McLeod Bethune, a prior suffragist, an educator and leader in the National Association of Colored Women. When Mrs. Bethune, the only black woman in attendance, enters the dining room it is Sara Roosevelt who gets up to greet her.

Sara has come some distance of her own toward having respect for African Americans. Mrs. Bethune relates, "That grand old lady took my arm and seated me to the right of Eleanor Roosevelt in the seat of honor! I can remember, too, how the faces of the Negro servants lit up with pride when they saw me seated at the center of that imposing gathering…"[7]

A terrible custom that is still unchallenged well into the 1930s is the right of whites to torture and kill African Americans. In the year 1933 alone, there are 28 lynchings. In fact, from the 1880s through the 1950s there are over 5,000 lynching murders and not one conviction.

When Eleanor becomes First Lady in 1933, she is constantly updating Franklin

Postcard depicting the lynching of Lige Daniels, in Center, Texas, USA, August 3, 1920

on the unconstitutional treatment of African Americans and is pushing for an anti-lynching law. It is a slow uphill battle since Franklin doesn't want to offend the southern Democratic white voters.

To stop this turning a blind eye by the feds and to pressure the government to uphold the constitutional rights for all of its citizens the National Association for the Advancement of Colored People (NAACP) was established in 1909. Walter White is head of the NAACP at the time that Franklin is president and Mr. White is in constant touch with Eleanor.

Eleanor is again urging Franklin to support the anti-lynching bill, but Franklin refuses and uses the excuse of not wanting to violate states' rights. The real reason is Northern Democrats did not want to antagonize Southern Democrats and thereby lose their votes or lose power to the Republicans. The north also has its own levels of racial hatred with its equal level of self-serving stubbornness to change.

In 1933, Mr. White sends Eleanor a full report of the most recent lynching of a man, Claude Neal. The lynching, announced ahead of time in newspapers and on the radio, leads to thousands showing up to watch and participate. The event is horrific.

As General Patton would make the local Germans go to the concentration camp to bear witness to the atrocities committed to the Jews, Walter White sends this eyewitness account to Eleanor.

"After taking the nigger to the woods about four miles from Greenwood, they cut off his penis. He was made to eat it. They cut off his testicles and made him eat them and say he liked it. ...

Then they sliced his sides and stomach with knives and every now and then somebody would cut off a finger or toe. Red hot irons were used on the nigger to burn him from top to bottom.

From time to time during the torture a rope was tied around Neal's neck, and he was pulled up over a limb and held there until he almost choked to death. Then he was let down, and the torture began all over again. After several hours of this unspeakable torture, they decided just to kill him.

Neal's body was tied to a rope on the rear of an automobile and dragged over the highway to the Cannidy home. Here a mob, estimated to number somewhere between 3000 and 7000 people from eleven southern states, was excitedly waiting his arrival. When the car which was dragging Neal's body came in front of the Cannidy home, a man who was riding the rear bumper cut the rope.

A woman came out of the Cannidy house and drove a butcher knife into his heart. Then the crowd came by and some kicked him and some drove their cars over him.

Men, women, and children were numbered in the vast throng that came to witness the lynching. It is reported from reliable sources that the little children, some of them mere tots, who lived in the Greenwood neighborhood, waited with sharpened sticks for the return of Neal's body, and that when it rolled in the dust on the road that awful night, these little children drove their weapons deep into the flesh of the dead man.

The body, which by this time was horribly mutilated, was taken to Marianna, a distance of ten or eleven miles, where it was hung to a tree on the northeast corner of the courthouse square. Pictures were taken of the mutilated form and hundreds of photographs were sold for fifty cents each. Scores of citizens viewed the body as it hung in the square. The body was perfectly nude until the early morning when someone had the decency to hang a burlap sack over the middle of the body. The body was cut down about eight-thirty Saturday morning, October 27, 1934.

Fingers and toes from Neal's body have been exhibited as souvenirs in Marianna where one man offered to divide the finger which he had with a friend as "a special favor." Another man has one of the fingers preserved in alcohol.

When Mr. White asks Eleanor why the president doesn't speak out against lynching during the address to Congress later that year, Eleanor writes to White this hollow response, "He wants me to say that he was talking to the leaders on the lynching question and his sentence on crime in his address to Congress touched on that because lynching is a crime."[9]

White also asks Eleanor to speak at a protest meeting. Franklin tells Eleanor 'no' and Eleanor complies.

Discussions on whether Eleanor could have done more are valid. It should be remembered; she might have a front row seats at the political game, but she is not in the position of a political player to change laws. She must also keep open her small window of opportunity to speak with the president.

Eleanor is sickened by these atrocities that are brazenly committed, not in the shadows of our society but often in broad daylight. She is determined to challenge the entire structure of America's segregated life. To do this she changes strategy. Rather than go to the president she goes to the people. What she can do is raise the pressure through increased public awareness so the citizens, not the politicians, will demand change.

The following are examples of what she did. For every one of these stories there are pages more folded away in biographies and historical archives that describe her fight for the end to racial violence and equal rights for all Americans.

In the spring of 1934, she helps organize The Washington Conference on Negro Education. Eleanor, as a speaker says,

"I think the day of selfishness is over; the day of really working together has come, and we must learn to work together all of us, regardless of race or creed or color… We go ahead together or we go down together…"[10]

That same year she also helps organize the National Conference on Fundamental Problems in the Education of Negroes. Her bold speech, which is broadcast nationwide, includes, "I noticed in the papers this morning the figures given of the cost in certain states per capita for the education of a colored child and of a white child, and I could not help but think … how stupid we are…" and "There are many people in this country, many white people, who have not had the opportunity for education… and there are also many Negroes who have not had the opportunity… Both these conditions should be remedied and the same opportunities should be accorded to every child regardless of race or creed…"[11]

"Wherever the standard of education is low, the standard of living is low."[12]

Some of the population is suggesting that 'Negroes' should just be happy with what they have, and educating them will only make them ask for more. But Eleanor counters this foolishness with the argument, "To deny any part of a population the opportunities for more enjoyment in life, for higher aspirations, is a menace to the nation as a whole. There has been too much concentrating wealth, and even if it means that some of us have got to learn to be a little more unselfish about sharing what we have than we have in the past, we must realize that it will profit us all in the long run."[13] (Eleanor applies this to herself. For years she gives away most of her earnings from lectures and writing to support the causes for which she is fighting.)

Eleanor encourages the public to open their eyes and see that this injustice is a matter of their own national security.

"The nation cannot expect the colored people to feel that the U.S. is worth defending if they continue to be treated as they are treated now."[14] This argument will be even stronger when later in the U.N. it is difficult for the U.S. to expect Russia to uphold any human rights standards when Russia can point to our own blatant disregard for the human rights of African Americans.

She opposes the Navy policy which keeps its African American enlistees in the servile support jobs of mess stewards, cooks, waiters, etc. When an angry man accuses Eleanor of agitating the races to push for more, she responds, "I am not agitating the race question. The race question is agitated because people will not act justly and fairly toward each other as human beings."[15] And she more than once reminds these accusers, "…you must remember that the President is their President also."[16]

Eleanor's words that apply to African Americans fighting for our country are timeless and could apply to the current drama of accepting gays in the military. She writes in her column, "I wonder if I can transmit to you the feeling which I have so strongly. In a nation such as ours, every man who fights for us is in some way, our man. His parents may be of any race or religion, but if that man dies, side by side with all of his buddies, and if your heart is with any man, in some way it must be with all."[17]

On the home front, she pushes the Democratic Party to make the New Deal policies open for African Americans and vote for the anti-lynching laws. To leverage her cause, she points out how the Republicans use this glaring weakness against the Democrats. They point out, "Five thousand Americans have been lynched in the last fifty years in this great free country of ours that is supposed to be the most civilized in the world.

The rest of the world laughs at us every time we say we stand for justice and law and order…" (Speech by Hamilton Fish)[18]

This point of the national reputation is well taken and referred to even by Hitler. In 1933 he states, "We merely wish to state that the United States possesses rigorous immigration laws while Germany has absolutely none thus far. We further point to American relations with Negroes—social and political."[19] When the Nazis see Franklin not fight for anti-lynching or stop-segregation-laws, they feel safe to announce a national boycott of Jewish businesses and professions.[20]

How can the United States issue any statement of condemnation to Germany when we are the ones murdering African American citizens just for wanting to vote?

So Eleanor can be credited with being one of the first to recognize the global impact of denying categories of our American citizens their rights. She worries that we will be, "on a par with Nazism which we fight and makes us tremble for what human beings may do when they no longer think but feel themselves be dominated by their worst emotions."[21]

When unthinking emotions are aroused, we usually find that whatever prejudices are held are channeled by the emotions into expressions that had nothing to do with reality but simply are an outlet for the prejudices."[22] Eleanor writes in her "My Day" column, 1962

Eleanor is also insisting that the law 'separate but equal' is not right. "The basic fact of segregation which warps and twists the lives of our Negro population was itself discriminatory."[23] Eleanor starts integrating wherever possible. Much to the dismay of her Hudson Valley neighbors, this includes them.

When a few of these elite ladies are asked to lunch at Eleanor's Val-Kill home, they are pleased to think they will be sipping tea with one of their own who happens to be First Lady to the United States. They are stunned by what happens next. One of the women reports, "We thought it would be a nice small intimate party and give us a chance to talk with Eleanor. Before we knew it, a delegation of two hundred ladies arrived— colored."[24]

When Eleanor visits Franklin at his home in Warm Springs, Georgia, the white residents are not fond of Eleanor and quickly acknowledge, "We didn't like her a bit; she ruined every maid we ever had."[25]

This southern sentiment held true for some citizens in Birmingham, Alabama too. In November 1938, Eleanor is the keynote speaker for the biracial Southern Conference on Human Welfare. Police official, Eugene "Bull" Conner (infamous for his later part in the Birmingham Riots and arresting Martin Luther King Jr.) hears African Americans and whites are sitting side by side in the audience. He comes to the conference each day to enforce the law of segregation. Eleanor, not wanting to relinquish the fight by sitting on the white side, takes a folding chair and sits in the aisle.[26]

The absurd shrillness of the white's fear of 'mixing' is apparent when the South uses as evidence of Eleanor's impropriety, a Detroit photo of Eleanor shown with an African American. Is Eleanor kissing this person? Holding hands with this person? Dancing? No. The photo is of Eleanor leaning over and smiling at a small African American girl. The child is handing Eleanor a bouquet of

1984 Stamp

flowers. [To commemorate the improvement in society's attitude this photo went on to become a 32 cent stamp in 1984.]

Eleanor's simple gracious act garners this response from the African American community, "They know not what they do, these race baiters and exploiters of unreason. And you render deep service to the enduring values of civilization by serving the nation as an historic example of simple humanity… in the highest place."[27]

In contrast are letters from the white end of the spectrum, "The influence you are having on the Negroes may do great harm to this nation. You are making them feel they are equal to the white race … You may not believe in amalgamation of the races, but they do not know that…"[28]

When the north and south are looking to blame someone for the race riots in Detroit the summer of 1943 *The Jackson Daily News* writes that Eleanor is "morally responsible" for the riot and, "It is blood on your hands, Mrs. Roosevelt." Adding, "You have been personally proclaiming and practicing social equality at the White House and wherever you go, Mrs. Roosevelt. What followed is not history." A resident of Detroit writes to the president, "It is my belief, Mrs. Roosevelt and Mayor Jeffries of Detroit are somewhat guilty of the race riots due to their coddling of negroes."[29]

As the First Lady, Eleanor showcases a variety of artists to give concerts at the White House. In 1936 this includes the world famous contralto Marian Anderson, an African American. Three years later, the Daughters of the American Revolution (DAR) deny Marian Anderson permission to sing for an integrated audience at the Constitution Hall. Eleanor, a member of the

DAR, resigns. She does this as a public protest. What Eleanor writes in her column shows the considerations of her decision.

"The question is, if you belong to an organization and disapprove of an action which is typical of a policy, shall you resign or is it better to work for a changed point of view within the organization? In the past, when I was able to work actively in any organization to which I belonged, I have usually stayed in until I had at least made a fight and been defeated. Even then, I have as a rule accepted my defeat and decided either that I was wrong or that I was perhaps a little too far ahead of the thinking of the majority of that time. I have often found that the thing in which I was interested was done some years later. But, in this case I belong to an organization in which I can do no active work. They have taken an action which has been widely talked of in the press. To remain as a member implies approval of that action, and therefore I am resigning."[30]

Eleanor's scheme is to increase public awareness and bring about change through the citizens. Not only is she achieving this goal but after her DAR resignation, a Gallup poll shows that Eleanor has a 67 percent approval rating.

Marian Anderson goes on to perform at an open air concert on the steps of the Lincoln Memorial for a crowd of 75,000 people. Amidst threats on her life, Ms. Anderson is unafraid to sing the poignant words:…

My country, 'tis of thee,
Sweet land of liberty,
Of thee I sing;
Land where my fathers died,
Land of the pilgrims' pride
From every mountainside,
Let freedom ring.

**Eleanor Roosevelt and Mirian Anderson
at a later meeting in Japan**

Eleanor has given the event her support, and yet chooses not to attend. This author hopes she regretted that decision.

Eleanor's weekly column is relentless in striving to educate and enlighten. She asks her readers whether they could appreciate being forced to use segregated hospital facilities of lesser quality, "Suppose we white people were taken ill in those areas of the world, and this type of segregation were practiced against us?"[31]

Her point blank tactics can be unnerving to perpetrators who are caught on her radar. She spares no punches when she says, "I can only say I felt mortified that in the North we still have a club, the West Side Tennis Club, which is not ashamed to say that it bars Jews and Negroes from membership." "But how can we in the North ask of the South the sacrifices that we are now asking if we countenance this kind of snobbish discrimination? If you can't play tennis with Negroes, how come you are willing to let them be drafted into your army and die for you? I am ashamed for my white people. I am one of them, and their stupidity and cruelty make me cringe."[32]

She also uses her column to voice her appreciation. "I would like to speak in praise of those white people in the South who have long fought for the rights of all their fellow citizens. They are probably being made to suffer more than any of us in the North can imagine at the present time."[33]

The fifties, the days of sit-ins and boycotts, Eleanor says, "I think everyone must be impressed by the dignity and calmness with which the boycott of the bus companies in Montgomery, Alabama has been carried on by the Negroes. Gandhi's theory of nonviolence seems to have been learned very well."[34]

Eleanor's role in desegregation also applies to guests at the White House. She expects her seamstress, an African American woman, to come through the front door. She invites a group of 60 girls, the majority being African American, to a garden party. When Eleanor's personal friend, Mary McCleod Bethune is coming up the sidewalk, Eleanor goes out to greet her, kissing her cheek and taking her arm.

Eleanor helps finance and promotes summer seminars and camps for African American girls. She writes letters of recommendation for African Americans to be appointed to jobs and when Franklin has a new school for white children built in Warm Springs, Eleanor helps raise money for a school for the African American children of Warm Springs.

In 1950 Eleanor is pleased to announce, "In the future the blood donor card will no longer designate whether blood given is White, Negro or Oriental. The Board of Governors announced this decision. Scientists have been urging this for some time, since it is a well known fact that human blood is alike, regardless of race."[35]

She understands and lives by her words, "human beings had rights as human beings."[36]

Women's Rights

"The battle for the individual rights of women is one of long standing and none of us should countenance anything which undermines it." This quote by Eleanor is a far cry from where she started.

In 1911 Eleanor shows no interest in being a part of the Women's Suffrage movement until she hears that Franklin has joined. Her response is, "somewhat shocked, as I had never given the question serious thought." At this time she "took for granted that men were superior creatures and still knew more about politics than women." So she decides, "I realized that if my husband were a suffragist I probably must be too."[37]

In 1913 the women's suffrage movement stages a parade in conjunction with Wilson's inauguration. Eleanor can do her share of belittling when she writes to a friend, "The suffrage parade was too funny and nice fat ladies with bare legs and feet exposed...."[38]

After the dual crisis of the Mercer affair and Franklin's polio, Eleanor has slowly reformed herself from a desire to appease to being authentic. The National Consumers League, the National League of Women Voters, and the National Woman's Party are just a few of the organizations Eleanor is a part of as she begins to advocate against discriminatory practices.

As her own perspective of women's issues changes, she states, "If we are still a negligible factor, ignored and neglected, we must be prepared to admit in what we have ourselves failed."[39] Eleanor encourages women to stay informed so their opinions are not just "a reaction to propaganda."[40] As early as the 1920s (women had just gotten the right to vote in August 1920) Eleanor is writing articles to demand real power for women. She felt women got into politics to make things better for most people while men got involved to play politics and win elections.[41]

Suffrage Parade, 1913, Library of Congress

Eleanor's willingness to use the media goes against her upbringing that advocates women stay out of any publicity. Eleanor recalled, "It was hard for me at first. I was brought up by a very strict grandmother who thought no lady should ever have stories written about her, except in the society columns."[42]

Picketing the White House, 1917

Public opinion and male domination are slow to change especially in light of economic downturn, the Depression. Several programs that are part of the federal New Deal are actually a set back to the progress of women in the work place. The National Recovery Act institutes lower wages for women.[43] The Economy Act in 1933 mandates that all federally employed women married to federally employed men can be fired. This means they lose all rights to reappointment and to any pension to which they have been contributing.[44] States followed suit to increase jobs for men. The states pass laws to fire and ban women who are married school teachers, university professors and hospital workers.[45]

Eleanor uses her radio addresses and her daily newspaper column to not only educate the women but for them to educate her. When she starts her column she tells her readers, "I want you to write to me." And "even if your views clash with what you believe to be my views." In six months she receives 301,000 letters. She takes time to listen to their problems and every night answers many of the letters herself.

In a 1933 press conference she tells women, "have a special stake in watching national and international news. Every woman should have a knowledge of what is going on [in London]. It does affect the future amicable relations between the nations of the world. It has been stated that the debt question is not to be discussed. But whatever does come out will be vitally important to every woman in her own home."[46]

She advises women, "Get into the game and stay in it. Throwing mud from the outside won't help. Building up from the inside will."[47]

"Too often the great decisions are originated and given form in bodies made up wholly of men, or so completely dominated by them that whatever of special value women have to offer is shunted aside without expression."[48]

In her later years, as a U.N. delegate, Eleanor says, "So against odds, the women inch forward…" although she declares, "but I'm rather old to be carrying on this fight!"[49]

American Jews

Eleanor's progress toward publicly supporting the rights of Jews is also a slow process of untangling her own prejudices.

In 1918, when she and Franklin are living in Washington, they are invited to a party to honor Bernard Baruch, a Jew. Eleanor writes to Sara, "I'd rather be hung than seen at" the party, and afterward writes to tell her, "The Jew party was appalling."[50] This is the same Bernard Baruch she later loves and admires. By 1930 she enjoys dancing with him and considers him, "one of the wisest and most generous people I have ever known." And she writes to him, "There are few people one trusts without reservation in life and I am deeply grateful to call you that kind of a friend."[51]

The United States government must also untangle its prejudice, but it won't be in time to save the millions of Jews who are being murdered in Germany. Anti-Semitism is not the only reason for U.S. inaction. As mentioned earlier, it's awkward for our country to point an accusing finger at Germany when our own country is turning a blind eye to its African American citizens being lynched every month.

Like placating a bully, this works to Hitler's advantage. In April 1933 Hitler says, "Through its immigration law America has inhibited the unwelcome influx of such races as it has been unable to tolerate."[52]

Eleanor is hard pressed to argue with this. Her public response is, "What has happened to our country? If we study our own history, we find that we have always been ready to receive the unfortunates from other countries, and though this may seem a generous gesture on our part, we have profited a thousand fold by what they have brought us."[53]

On April 1, 1933, the boycott which was announced by the National Socialistic Party began. Placard reads, "Germans, defend yourselves, do not buy from Jews." Placed at the Jewish Tietz store, Berlin.
Credits: National Archives

Eleanor receives a letter in December 1933 from a woman with information of what is happening to the Jews in Germany. Eleanor writes back, "Unfortunately, in my present position, I am obliged to leave all contacts with foreign governments in the hands of my husband and his advisors."[54]

If Eleanor wants to keep any inroads of communication to the president, she has to abide by the rules he has given her. Franklin has told her to stay out of international affairs. Eleanor's compliance may seem weak, but she does pass information on to Franklin. Ignoring the wise cracks and criticism from Franklin's inner circle, she follows up with a stream of notes and keeps nudging Franklin to take action. Eleanor also works within immigration laws to have Jewish children allowed into the United States. To the shame of our nation, this effort is struck down. However, nothing can strike down the determination of this First Lady.

It's 1938 and the United States will not be involved in WWII for close to four more years. The U.S. is still refusing to acknowledge there are German death camps for the Jews, and Eleanor is becoming more outspoken on anti-Semitism. Where she had earlier resigned in silence from a club that excluded a Jewish friend of hers, now in 1938, discovering the country club where she is to speak has a "no Jews allowed" policy, she makes a public statement that she will decline the speaking engagement.[55]

Eleanor helps establish a home for immigrant Jewish girls in Jerusalem in 1937. In 1938 she helps promote the settlement of one thousand Jewish refugee families. Eleanor also steps up her advocacy for tolerance, by continuing to educate her reading audience. In November 1938 she writes that "the present catastrophe for Jew and Gentile alike … In books … schools, newspapers, plays, assemblies, we want incessant truth telling about these old legends that divide and antagonize and waste us." And she notes that it is beyond her understanding "the kind of racial and religious intolerance which is sweeping the world today."[56]

Eleanor had not always understood the desire of Jews to have their own country [Zionism]. She thought they should just assimilate into the country and culture where they live. After the war Eleanor voices her support of establishing a homeland for the Jewish people. She has realized, "the horror of their situation is what makes it tragic, because those who are being kept out of Palestine are the waifs and strays of horror camps." And she will even say about U.S. policies, "...but I deplore even more the attitude of self-righteous governments. Our own Government position has never gone beyond pious hopes and unctuous words."[57]

German civilians, under direction of U.S. medical officers, walk past a group of 30 Jewish women starved to death by SS troops in a 300 mile march across Czechoslovakia

When Eleanor goes to Europe after WWII, she visits the concentration camps. She could have stayed away, aloof in formalities that are befitting a former First Lady, but she wants to bear witness to what has happened. She says they were the "saddest places…the Jewish camps particularly are things I will never forget."

This anguish is overwhelming as she discovers that thousands of Jews are now being held in detention camps with other Germans. Great Briton, who is governing Palestine, wants to appease the Arabs (oil) and so has placed severe restrictions on Jews immigrating to Palestine. Eleanor says, "The thought of what it must mean to those poor human beings seems almost unbearable. They have gone through so much hardship and had thought themselves free forever from Germany, the country they associate with concentration camps and crematories. Now they are back there again. Somehow it is too horrible for any of us in this country to understand."[58]

"The weight of human misery here in Europe is something one can't get out of one's heart."[59] One third of the world's Jewish population has been exterminated.

For some, this wretched situation leads to a protective blank stare of disbelief because to understand this mass cruelty, one will jump off the cliff of despair. This is not Eleanor's choice. For a woman who cannot walk by a homeless person without feeling their hunger, taking in the extent of this human depravity takes broad shoulders, a large heart and a vision that can see past this wretched evidence to a people and time that can be better. Eleanor 'can't get out of one's heart' this memory and it will carry her through the coming years when she makes her finest contribution to the world.

**Two men sitting after liberation from
Lager-Norhausen Death Camp, Germany, 1945**

8
WAR

Eleanor's generation fights through World War I and its sequel, World War II. No one feels assured there won't be a World War III.

During WWI, Eleanor volunteers every week with the Red Cross and visits the veterans in hospitals. She sees firsthand not only the mutilated arms, legs, and faces of men but those whose sanity has cracked under the strain of battle. She visits St. Elizabeth's hospital where the Navy has an installation for young men who have gone temporarily or permanently insane.

Eleanor relates, "It was a long ward with men, some of them in cubicles chained to their beds, and a strange sound permeating the whole place. The men were talking and mumbling to themselves, not conversation, just private thoughts revealed in an endless series of monologues. At the end of the ward, standing where the sun coming through the window touched his golden hair, stood a handsome young man. He did not see us. He saw nothing but some private vision of his own. He kept muttering.

"What is he saying?" I asked the doctor.

"He keeps repeating the orders at Dunkirk to go to the shelters."

"Will he get over it?"

"I don't know," the doctor said flatly.

"I watched the boy struggling with his private hell …"[1]

After WWI Eleanor visits cemeteries in France witnessing the miles of parallel white markers, graves for the dead. In twenty five years, at the end of WWII, she will be back again, paying her respects to more fresh graves, thousands of them.

As Europe is being overrun with Nazi armies many Americans want to stay with their isolationist stand and pacify Hitler's demands. To this Eleanor responds, "Appeasement does not work where ethics do not exist."[2] Many of Eleanor's supporters feel betrayed by her backing the war. She tells them, "I don't want to go to war. But war may come to us."[3]

Attack on Pearl Harbor

When the United States is attacked at Pearl Harbor, December 7, 1941, Eleanor's words come true—war came to us.

"I am afraid that I am a very realistic pacifist... We can only disarm with other nations; we cannot disarm alone."[5]

There are still critics of the war and they say to Eleanor, "The man who goes to war for an ideal sacrifices his ideals in the process." Eleanor responds, "I agree with you in theory, but I would rather die than submit to rule by Hitler and Stalin, would not you?"[4]

"You use every means in your power to prevent a fight, and this includes giving all the assistance you possibly can, short of military assistance... But if war comes to your own country, then even pacifists... must stand up and fight for their beliefs."[6]

Eleanor Roosevelt talking with troops, Sydney Australia, 1943

During the war, Eleanor is continuing to support causes. She pushes for government contracts for minorities. Pleased that women are being hired for factory jobs, she advocates for day care at the facilities. To give the women time to shop for their homes, she pushes to have stores open extended hours. Her most prolific support is for the troops, and it would make even the stout of heart exhausted.

Eleanor visits the troops that are fighting in the Pacific. Riding on military flights is far from first class. There is no heat and the seating is uncomfortable; sleeping is impossible. One trip includes all of these stops: Hawaii, Christmas Island, Penryhn Island, Bora Bora, Aitutaki, Tutuila, Samoa, Fiji, New Caledonia; Auckland, Wellington, and Rotorua in New Zealand; Sydney, Canberra, Melbourne, Rockhampton, Cairns, Brisbane in Australia; Efate, Espiritu Santo, Guadalcanal and Wallis.

During these visits Eleanor wants to make the most of her time. For one particular 12 hour day she inspects two Navy hospitals, rides a boat to an officers' rest home, goes to a luncheon, inspects one Army hospital, reviews the 2nd Marine Raider Battalion,

Eleanor Roosevelt, General Harmon, and Admiral Halsey, in front of 'her' plane, 1943

makes a speech at the Service Club, attends a reception and is the guest of honor at a dinner. When she inspects a hospital, this means she greets all the patients, the kitchen staff, and officers. Service members give her letters to take back or requests for Eleanor to get in touch with their mothers. She does.

To decrease formalities and simplify her wardrobe, her role on the trips is not as First Lady but a representative of the Red Cross. Late nights are spent writing reports about facilities and conditions. These reports are sent back to the Red Cross. Before turning in she also writes her "My Day" column to be wired back to the states the next morning.

At one stop she hears the troops are heading out for the front. Knowing that for many this may be their last day alive she insists on being driven out to meet them. She walks to each truck load and wishes the boys good luck. On that day, Eleanor's unpretentious ways make her every soldier's mother. Upholding the unwritten rule, "Don't cry in front of the boys," she bids them each farewell. Although those with Eleanor report, "her voice quavered."[7]

The Commander of the South Pacific, Admiral Halsey, thinks visits from dignitaries are nothing but a nuisance. He changes his mind when it comes to Eleanor. In his report he states she, "went into every ward, stopped at every bed, and spoke with every patient... she walked for miles, and she saw patients who were grievously and gruesomely wounded. But I marveled most at their expressions as she leaned over them. It was a sight I will never forget."[9] This crusty warrior went on to say, "I was ashamed of my original surliness. She alone

"The loss of a generation makes itself felt acutely twenty to thirty five years later, when many men who would have been leaders are not there to lead."[8] Eleanor writes this the summer 1929

had accomplished more good than any other person or any group of civilians, who had passed through my area..."[10]

Eleanor's genuine concern makes each visit meaningful. This example is only one of hundreds of accounts of her personal attention to help the soldiers. At her stop on Christmas Island, she visits one young man because the doctor is worried about his will to live. She relates this in her autobiography, "I made him promise that he would try to get well if I would try to see his mother on my return. I did see her, and fortunately he recovered and came to see me when he got back to the United States."[11]

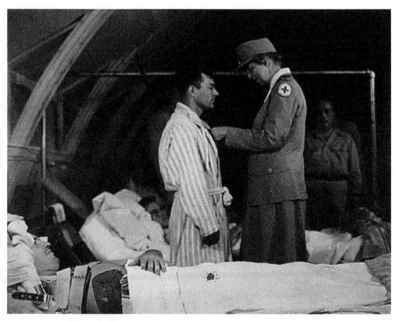

Eleanor Roosevelt, Santo, South Pacific, 1943

Having witnessed so much pain and suffering, Eleanor's response to news that the war has ended in Europe is tempered. "I cannot feel a spirit of celebration today. I am glad that our men are no longer going to be shot at and killed in Europe, but the war in the Pacific still goes on. Men are dying there, even as I write. It is far more a day of dedication for us, a day on which to promise that we will do our utmost to end war and build peace. Some of my own sons, with millions of others, are still in danger."[12]

Without definitive plans for peace, she worried more war would come. She said in her "My Day" column, "I remembered the way the people demonstrated when the last war ended, (WWI) but I felt this time that the weight of suffering which has engulfed the world during so many years could not so quickly be wiped out."[13]

Bearing in mind the emotional grief in the thousands of homes now empty of loved ones, she also reminds her readers that in the midst of celebrating the war's end, "One cannot forget, however the many, many people to whom this day will bring a keener sense of loss, for as others come home, their loved ones will not return."[14]

For these sacrifices not to be in vain Eleanor says, "The men who fought this war are entitled to a chance to build a lasting peace."[15]

The body count of American casualties in the last eighty years is two million. Add to this the news reels of the Nazi death camps which lead people to question any hope for our humanity. A wave of cynicism has people asking, "So when is World War III?".

Part Two — Awakening
Reflections for the Reader

In *Rocky,* the Italian Stallion bloodied from his fight, wins the real fight, which is within himself. He cries out from the boxing ring to his beloved Adrian. He doesn't care what anyone else thinks. He dares to bare his heart.

Eleanor has been emotionally beat up with betrayal. Society had ring side seats so her humiliation is public. The fight is not with Franklin or society. The battle is within herself—to be what she wants to be.

In order to do this, she must first choose to let go of her victim story.

Cinderella had an advantage. She was beautiful.

"No one can make you feel inferior without your consent."

Eleanor said those words and she lived up to those words. She was going to live her own way. This was more risky since she is not Cinderella pretty.

Eleanor has freed herself from the fear of society's expectations. Her continual acts of compassion, some might judge foolhardy. She advocates for causes with no regard for society's scorn.

The true test of character is applying the lessons learned.

General Patton has the famous line for the United States Third Army "Now I want you to remember that no bastard ever won a war by dying for his country. You won it by making the other poor dumb bastard die for his country."

Patton wanted to take the glory out of dying in war.

Eleanor wanted to take the glory out of war.

PART THREE

POLITICAL, PUBLIC & PERSONAL STORMS

FLASH

Context and Comments

In a theater musical there is often a scene where characters are singing several songs at once. The contrast of melodies, representing their conflicting points of view, fuels the exquisite harmony as their voices tumble and climax over each other. This artistic portrayal of the drama works beautifully on stage. If only it could be that melodious in life.

Political Storms

Jingo: a person who is a belligerent nationalist, one who boasts of patriotism and favors an aggressive foreign policy

During the 1930s and into the late 1950s there is legitimate concern about the world-wide spread of Communism. The shrill fear tactics of Republicans is warping the public dialogue. The lead role is Republican Senator Joe McCarthy, a jingo. Claiming that Communism, which had started in Russia (the Red Scare), has come to America, they infer the people are just a little bit 'Red.' Using a grim play on words, suspects are labeled 'Pinkos.'

Willfully blind to inequalities in our democracy, they ignore the perspective of an African-American veteran, returning from WWII. He has just finished fighting for freedom and democracy for a government that is now refusing his right to housing, a job, voting, or service at a restaurant. Any discussion for why Communism is a viable option for disenfranchised citizens is met with indignant accusations of being un-American.

With distorted innuendoes and pugnacious fervor, later called McCarthyism, Senator McCarthy is scrambling to compile evidence and make his case. By dredging up outdated reports, the reputations and careers of thousands of Americans are ruined (blacklisted) because old records documenting when someone attended minor activities or talked to members of the Communist party are used as evidence of 'Un-American Activities.' McCarthy puts Eleanor at the top of his list.

Public Storms

"… the crushing weight of an entire society whose masculine laws and orientations stifle the voices and the emotional needs of women."[1] is a biographer's apt description of the climate for women. Violent threats to women who choose to address the inequalities are found in the words of play critic Nathanael West who writes about women, "… what they all needed was a good rape."[2] Not as threatening but clearly dismissive, John Crowe Ransom voices his description of the woman's role, "A woman lives for love … safer as a biological organism, she remains fixed in her famous attitudes, and is indifferent to intellectuality."[3]

If women express their honest opinion about sex as Elizabeth Cady Stanton did in the late 1800s, "a healthy woman has as much passion as a man" or Kate Chopin writing about women coming to know their own physical pleasures, the public is shocked.[4] Eleanor contends, "Men have to be humored. I know that men have to believe that they are superior to women, and women from the time they are little girls have to learn self-discipline because they have to please the gentlemen. They have to manage some man all their lives."[5]

In this world where women gain influence through charm and sex appeal, Eleanor and her friends refuse the role of a 'flapper princess' or today it would be called 'eye candy.' Being direct in their opinions and not diminishing their intelligence they are breaking the rules. Like throwing back the curtain from the Wizard of Oz, the entrenched "Boys Club," doesn't appreciate being exposed. Their diversionary trick of counter accusations (Eleanor is priggish, a she-man, cold and unforgiving) has been used by critics and historians to provide cover for the Club to regroup and adjust the curtain.

To this day, current documentaries on the History Channel trot out the one quote that Eleanor supposedly said to her daughter, 'that sex is to be endured.' If Eleanor did say this, it's quite possible it was an offhand joke or her way of inferring Franklin was a bad lover. Instead, this one comment is used as evidence in support of the "Boys Club" perspective that Franklin's philandering was Eleanor's fault.

Personal Storms

Aside from political attacks and Eleanor's fight to redefine herself as a woman, Eleanor must also consider her role as a mother. What would be the normal strife and conflict for a family with five children is compounded by the father's crippling disease of Polio. How can the impact be measured? The children, once able to romp and tussle with their father, now take careful steps as he leans on them to walk.

The children's mixed sympathies and adoration of their father is fueled by several other factors; their doting Grandmother Sara continues to be Franklin's biggest fan, society's no-fault fathering perspective is in full swing and something few families have to deal with—their father is President.

For the Roosevelt children, it is understandable they are unable to throw off such powerful blinders. However, they rarely grant Eleanor the same grace and understanding they so easily shower on their father.

Eleanor takes great pains to protect the privacy of her family. Large segments of her personal correspondence have disappeared. Who can blame her? No family is without its stories they would rather not have publicized. Adam and Eve would have preferred to not have recorded one of their sons murdered the other.

Information is relayed here, not as ammunition for a smug person to take verbal pot shots at the family. It is to show the complexities of a real life.

9

CRITICS

No one is above suspicion in the McCarthy era. Even Eisenhower, the American Five Star General, Supreme Allied Commander of the European Forces, is being investigated. If they go after Eisenhower, then, it comes as no surprise that Eleanor will also be a target. What should come as a surprise is Eisenhower never makes a public stand against the lies and fear-hawking of Joe McCarthy. Eleanor does.

When she finds out there is a move afoot to impugn the patriotism of Eisenhower, she writes in her "My Day" column that a "…group was formed the other day to prove that General Dwight D. Eisenhower is closely associated with Communists. This type of thing is becoming so ludicrous that each time it happens we should point it out and say to ourselves: 'How stupid can we be? Is hysterical fear turning us all into morons?'"[6]

Eleanor also says of McCarthy's scheming, "The day I'm afraid to sit down with people I do not know because five years from now someone will say five of those people were Communists, and therefore, you are a Communist—that will be a bad day. I want to be able to sit down with anyone who may have a new idea and not be afraid of contamination by association. In a democracy you must be able to meet with people and argue your point of view—people whom you have not screened beforehand. That must be a part of the freedom of people in the United States."[7]

As an outspoken woman, Eleanor is an easy target and being unattractive removes the protection that beauty provides. What could have been pictures of courage is instead caricatures of her protruding front teeth or mimicking her wavering voice. If that doesn't work for her adversaries, they use slander and character assassination.

A woman is like a tea bag, you never know how strong she is until she gets in hot water.
Eleanor Roosevelt

A journalist, Westbrook Pegler, writes about Eleanor at the height of McCarthyism, "The time has come to snatch this wily old conspirator (Eleanor) before Joe McCarthy's committee and chew her out… Joe McCarthy or Bill Jenner could tear her to tatters if either of them should ever drag her to the stand. She deserves far less respect than any conventional woman."[8] At one point Secretary of State Dulles calls Eleanor "more subversive and dangerous than Moscow."[9]

"I am indifferent to attacks on me, but I hate to see other people hurt. However I intend to go on fighting for the things in which I believe, and will undoubtedly furnish plenty of ammunition for attacks."[10]

Threats do not deter Eleanor from continuing her strong public statements. She calls McCarthy's bluff and responds that she would love to have the opportunity to come before the committee. McCarthy is the one to blink and does not respond.[11]

In spite of her 3,000 page FBI file on her 'un-American' activities, Eleanor doesn't buckle under the intimidation even when she is informed her hotel rooms are bugged. She continues to talk with and listen to people who carry other points of view, even if they are Communists. She fearlessly points out: "I have always believed ignorance was a sure way to fall a victim to propaganda. I do not believe in communism, because I do believe in freedom and in our form of government, but I did not attain that loyalty through repression."[12]

Being a visionary for peace and equality, Eleanor withstands the scoffing and does not succumb to watering down the message. "Sometimes I wonder if we will ever grow up in our politics and say definite things which mean something or whether we shall always go on using generalities to which everyone can subscribe, and which mean very little."[13]

Eleanor applies this to her opinions on party politics and is often reproved for not having a blind allegiance to the Democrats. She responds, "This is not disloyalty but will show that as members of a party they are loyal first to the fine things for which the party stands and when it rejects those things or forgets the legitimate objects for which parties exist, then as a party it cannot command the honest loyalty of its members."[14] Her briefer response is "… America must come first, not party."[15]

Eleanor's adversaries don't always stay leashed to their dogmatic responses. There are instances when she is acknowledged for her efforts, and some critics' opinions can change.

"Insincerity and sham, whether in men or in women, always fail in the end in public life."[16]

Going back to the year 1937, not only had Eleanor been elected as "outstanding woman of 1937" but an Ohio newspaper, *The Canton Repository*, is calling her, "the foremost individualist among all the First Ladies" and "she has lived her own life with a freedom that smashed precedent, traveling widely as she willed, speaking her own mind on every occasion and engaging in activities so diversified they are a little staggering."[17]

In 1938 for Eleanor's fifty-fourth birthday the *New York Times* reports, "This is not in the tradition of the wives of former Presidents. But she is so patently sincere and unpretentious in all she says and does, so ebulliently a part of every activity she undertakes, so good-humored even in the face of criticism, that she remains today one of the most popular women who ever lived in the White House. At 54 she could command a landslide of votes as Mrs. America."[18]

Lest it should be thought that women go easier on her, the initial opinion of a veteran journalist Rita S. Halle concerning Eleanor was "evidence of a ruthless craving for personal publicity." Later, Halle acknowledges, "a complete change of heart." And she went on to admire in Eleanor, "the magnetism of her simple sincerity."[19] At a dinner Halle listens as Eleanor "spoke of the needs of the common people, needs that could not be delayed for the unwinding of red tape, needs that she had seen with her own eyes, touched with the antennae of her own heart."[20]

When Eleanor visits England, she has dinner with Prime Minister and Mrs. Churchill. In the company of Winston Churchill, not many express a contrary perspective. Eleanor does. Making matters worse for Winston, during the course of conversation his wife agrees with Eleanor. Mrs.

"I'm a middle-aged woman. It's good to be middle-aged. Things don't matter so much. You don't take so hard when things happen to you that you don't like."[21]

Eleanor Roosevelt on her 48th birthday

Churchill leans over to Winston and says, "I think perhaps Mrs. Roosevelt is right." Mr. Churchill responds, "I have held certain beliefs for sixty years and I'm not going to change now."[22]

At the end of Eleanor's trip to England, Winston has his wife give Eleanor a hand written note saying, "You certainly have left golden footprints behind you."[23] And in the following year Churchill's admiration continues when he tells a friend that Eleanor has, "a spirit of steel and a heart of gold."[24]

10
REFUGE

Living against the wind is exhausting even for the stoutest of heart. Needing an escape from the scrutiny of the public eye is no surprise, and home is the place that comes to mind. Not for Eleanor.

As her public role has progressed, Eleanor's attempts at bringing home her personal confidence are thwarted. The undertow from Sara and Franklin is to maintain the old status quo. They are the ones to dole out family fun for the children. Eleanor's role is disciplinarian and bearing the blame for any family failure.

Franklin Jr. recalls, "Father had great difficulty in talking about anything purely personal or private....especially if it involved anything unpleasant. He left that to Mother."[2] When Eleanor asks Franklin to talk to two of their sons about drinking and

"I just want to tell you I haven't been ill at all. Something happened to me. I have gotten used to people who say they care for me but are only interested in getting to Franklin. But there was one person of whom I thought this was not true, that his affection was for me. I found this was not true and I couldn't take it."[1]

fast driving he does so with the preface, "Your mother tells me I must ask you to give me your license…"[3]

Adding to the swath of benevolent oversight is society's willingness to allow more lenient standards to the children of the president. When Franklin Jr. is stopped for speeding, the judge fines him thirty dollars and then takes him home for dinner.[4]

A luncheon with Sara at Springwood includes both Lord and Lady Astor, and Amelia Earhart. One of Sara's grandsons arrives unannounced. He needs money. Disregarding that his behavior is the direct result of her own training, Sara is annoyed. She steers the blame to Eleanor by telling the guests, "They never bother to telephone…But of course they have had no bringing up."[5]

Because the children are the president's, the press is quick to pick up the story that their son Elliot disappeared for three weeks leaving behind a wife and children. Eleanor writes to Hick, "And so news of our family is out and about." Historical records show Sara lays fault for Elliot's irresponsible behavior squarely at Eleanor's feet.[6]

Worn down by her mother-in-law's constant upper hand advantage, Eleanor writes to Hick, "My zest in life is rather gone for the time being. If anyone looks at me, I want to weep, … I get like this sometimes. It makes me feel like a dead weight, and my mind goes round and round like a squirrel in a cage. I want to run and I can't, and I despise myself. I can't get away from thinking about myself. Even though I know I'm a fool, I can't help it! … You are my rock, and I shall be so glad to see you Saturday night. I need you very much as a refuge just now."[8]

"… If I get sorry for myself, I'm no good to anybody else."[7]

Hick provides an intimate friendship where Eleanor is neither mocked nor maligned. During their camping trips through Yosemite, Eleanor takes special pleasure in her hiking stamina and horsemanship. Hick writes, "Climbing mountains … didn't bother her either. One morning she and the Chief Forest Ranger climbed up to an elevation of some 13,000 feet. …You'd have thought she had come in from a stroll in Central Park!"[10]

Eleanor's exhilaration is more than fresh air. Her exuberance is overcoming the uphill emotional climb to be the one to define herself. Years ago, on her honeymoon, she stayed back from the hike with Franklin. Now she would have raced to the top.

"Dear, it meant to so much to have even that little time with you and it does give me so much more than you know in a sense of closeness and warmth. I love you dearly."[9]

Eleanor Roosevelt on a horseback trip she took with Lorena Hickok, 1934

Striking out on her own trail has included setting up a household separate from Franklin. She has named the cottage after a nearby stream, Val-Kill. Of course, there is some interesting back story.

Eleanor resents living at Springwood and summers at Campobello, both being the domain of Sara. Even in the twin townhouse

Sara had built for them in New York City there are connecting doors on each floor to the adjoining townhouse where Sara resides. How disconcerting is it that Sara can 'appear' in Eleanor and Franklin's house at any time?

Franklin, never wanting to confront his mother, sees a way to appease the situation. On a few acres of the Hyde Park estate, Franklin has a home built for Eleanor and her two friends and co-owners Marion and Nan. Out from under Sara's halo of hubris, Val-Kill becomes Eleanor's place to entertain her own acquaintances.

By the 1930s there is a clear division between the households of Franklin and Eleanor. Franklin has his retreat home in Warm Springs, Georgia where he continues to hope the therapeutic waters will bring some relief to his legs.

Keeping a separate residence also frees Franklin to jockey in place his own version of 'The Boys Club.' Franklin enjoys society's support that membership for the ladies indicates their willingness to drink, gossip, and fawn over Franklin. Franklin will always have pretty and accommodating women even if it causes family division and not just with Eleanor.

"I don't think that Franklin likes women who think they are as good as he is."[1]

Betsey is their son James' wife. She has caught the eye of Franklin and he has her at his side to amuse and entertain him. James remembers, "Father approved because Betsey delighted him. She was pretty, playful, a teaser. She flattered him, and he adored her."[12] Franklin continues to have Betsey go with him, even to Warm Springs, overriding James' jealousy and in spite of the breakup of their marriage.

Eleanor, although willing to clap, admire, and dutifully attend political events as the spokesperson for Franklin, will not sell out and abide by this unwritten code of conduct in private settings. When it comes to Franklin's cocktail hours and parties, Eleanor writes to Hick, "… No, dear, we [Eleanor and Franklin] won't have scenes. I made up my mind to that last time, and I never have spoken to him about this but this burying things in your heart makes certain things look pretty odd in the future, and I think a little plain talk then will be a violent shock…"[13]

It is here we can finally have the 'plain talk.'

In the fight for equal rights, women are thrown in jail for peaceful picketing of the White House, spit on and attacked by police. When men bring Alice Paul, one of the imprisoned suffragists, before a psychologist the hope is to have her discredited by having her declared insane. To the doctor's credit he instead says, "Courage in women is often mistaken for insanity."

Eleanor, like so many women, is still tiptoeing around the elephant in the room. The conflict being ignored is the unspoken bargain that man's 'gift' of security is in exchange for the woman's vow of submission. Male control of money and marriage through the legal system ensures the elephant will stay while women learn to keep tossing peanuts as a means of garnering some leverage. For Eleanor it is just twenty years earlier when women had finally won the right to vote.

Eleanor speaks for many women who survive by the art of camouflage when she says, "So I learned self-discipline as a kind of defense. I learned to protect myself from disappointment by not asking for what I wanted."[14]

It is this self-discipline that is seen at the White House. It's the firm stance when her guard is up that makes her look stiff and awkward. It is a veiled look, so the turmoil of the heart is not revealed. Her pain from 1918 and continued conflict is obvious in several pictures with Franklin. The photos show a woman whose countenance is sadness and if her face is not turned away there is clearly a forlorn expression. Compare those to the hundreds of photos taken with her friends or at public events where she is free to be herself. Her radiant smile and sparkling eyes are easy evidence of assurance and joy.

**Franklin and Eleanor
New Years Ever, 1930**

Eleanor doesn't bother to contradict the misrepresentation of her being cold and distant. For all the causes she directly confronts, the double standards and inequalities of The Boys Club, is one fight in which she does not engage. Instead she turns to her refuge, Val-Kill.

Aside from the large cottage that Eleanor shares with Nan and Marion, they also build a second structure that is a woodworking factory to provide jobs for the local men and women. This operation is successful for about ten years. It closes because of the Depression in 1936. By this time Eleanor is First Lady and she converts that building into two apartments for herself and her secretary, Malvina "Tommy" Thompson. The upstairs is redone into bedrooms to accommodate a constant stream of guests and visiting grandchildren.

This getaway cottage with its outdoor pool and barbecue pit is a private setting where Eleanor can relax. It is where her body guard, Earl Miller, coaches her in target practice and diving. He buys Eleanor a horse and encourages her to get back to riding. Another gift is a police dog, Major, who Earl trains to protect 'his lady' as he refers to Eleanor.

Picnics and parties are always in the works as Eleanor revels in making her own plans with no intervention from Sara. Home movies, silly skits, reading poetry and serving drinks hardly line up with a portrayal of Eleanor being a drudge.

Earl remains Eleanor's personal friend for years but not her body guard. When Franklin wins the presidency, rather than bring Earl to D.C., Franklin has him reassigned to a job in New York. Eleanor could never have 'reassigned' any of the women in Franklin's attending court.

Earl Miller and Eleanor Roosevelt, 1934

Eleanor's son James, later in life, provides an honest assessment of Eleanor's affection for Earl. He "...gave her a great deal of what her husband and we, her sons, failed to give her. Above all, he made her feel that she was a woman."[15]

What Eleanor does take to the White House is her dog Major who snaps and growls at people. She also takes Mrs. Nesbitt, the cook who despises Franklin. According to one observer Mrs. Nesbitt had "contempt for the desires of the President." And "If he ordered something special, she just ignored it."[16] [Note: When naming the restaurant at the Home of Franklin D. Roosevelt National Historic Site, someone had a sense of humor. The restaurant is named Mrs. Nesbitt's Café.]

Franklin could have had Mrs. Nesbitt replaced. He had no qualms about sending Earl away or a different young male friend, more a surrogate son than potential lover, who was given orders to the Pacific. What might appear as idiosyncratic: Franklin's tolerance of Mrs. Nesbitt or Eleanor's snapping dog is merely representative of their underlying tug of war.

Eleanor's friendship with Marion and Nan becomes strained as Eleanor is expanding beyond their tutelage and bringing home new friends. Eleanor realizes her refuge is being compromised when she finds out that Marion and Nan are going to Franklin for chats about her. Eleanor's move into the remodeled factory building is a temporary fix.

The breaking point is a picnic that Eleanor is having that includes Franklin and over one hundred other people. Eleanor's brother Hall and his son go over to visit Marion and Nan who continue to serve Hall drinks, knowing his tendency to overwork the cocktail hour.[17]

As Hall's alcohol level increases the situation deteriorates. He wrestles with his son, breaks the child's clavicle and then insists on being the one to drive him to the hospital. Missing a curve in the road Hall crashes the car down an eight foot drop off. The police and ambulance are called.

Marion and Nan had put off crossing the lawn to tell Eleanor that trouble is brewing. It is after the accident when they inform her. Eleanor is hurt and furious.

Money, power, and prestige can't buy a refuge, even in this idyllic setting. Eleanor learns she must take charge of this situation if she is to have a place of sanctuary for herself. She makes the legal arrangements to buy out Marion and Nan. Val-Kill becomes Eleanor's domain.

Over the years, Val-Kill will be the informal setting to dignitaries such as Queen Wilhelmina, Nikita Khrushchev, Marshal Tito and John F. Kennedy. Picnics by the pool have home videos of Winston Churchill eating hotdogs.

Eleanor writes to her daughter Anna, "My house seems nicer than ever, and I could be happy in it alone! That's the last test of one's surroundings."

Amidst the drinking and eating, honest discussions and disagreements are encouraged and not seen as an attack on male virility. Eleanor does not need to use her maneuvering strategies to deal with Franklin and his entourage. To Franklin's credit, when he is visiting Val-Kill, he honors Eleanor's terms.

Val-Kill will stay Eleanor's safe haven, the only home she ever owns, until the end of her life.

11
BLINDSIDED BY FAMILY

On April 12, 1945 Franklin is in his fourth term as president. WWII is still raging, although it will be over this summer.

Franklin, trying to recoup, has been accompanied by a few female friends while staying at his home in Warm Springs, Georgia. He is deathly ill but able to sit for his portrait being painted. The artist has been commissioned by Lucy Mercer. Lucy is there with Franklin.

Eleanor is in Washington giving a speech. She gets a phone call earlier in the day that the president has fainted. The decision is that Eleanor should go ahead with her plans to avoid raising any public alarm and rumors. At the next meeting she gets the message that Franklin has died. She returns to the White House and prepares to fly immediately to Warm Springs.

Vice President Truman is called to the White House and sworn in as president. Offering his condolences to Eleanor he says, "Is there anything I can do for you?"

Truman records later her "deeply understanding" reply. Eleanor answers, "Is there anything we can do for you? For you are the one in trouble now."

Recognizing she is no longer First Lady, Eleanor asks if she might avail herself of a government plane to fly to Warm Springs. Truman, of course, says 'yes.'

That night at Warm Springs, wanting to hear exactly how Franklin died, Eleanor meets with Franklin's two cousins. Lucy has been shuttled away and Eleanor is not yet told about her. Eleanor goes in to the bedroom where the body of her husband lies.

In this personal moment of reflection, does she sigh in relief that his suffering is over, and the burden of world power no longer weighs on his shoulders? Is there a sigh for herself knowing that her suffering is over too? No longer having to disregard the sniggering as some woman moves to a more discreet distance from Franklin the minute Eleanor walks in the room? No longer the wrenching within when she hears the most virulent swipes on her character are coming from his staff? Do tears appear as she takes stock of their years spent in partnership that in spite of everything, she will miss him? Does she square her shoulders, readying for the onslaught of emotions from a country that has known Franklin as their leader for 13 years?

Who is there to give guidance on such an occasion? No one. Eleanor is in uncharted territory.

You gain strength, courage and confidence by every experience in which you really stop to look fear in the face. You are able to say to yourself, 'I have lived through this horror. I can take the next thing that comes along.' You must do the thing you think you cannot do.

Eleanor Roosevelt

After several minutes, Eleanor comes out of the room.

Eleanor is told that Franklin had been sitting for a portrait for Lucy and that Lucy had been there at the time of Franklin's death. Eleanor is also informed that her daughter Anna had helped coordinate not only this visit for Lucy but also several visits over the years to the White House. It was discreet of course. It was never when Eleanor was at the White House; only when she was out of town.

Eleanor might have had suspicions that Franklin still saw Lucy, but she was not prepared for the news that her daughter, Anna, had been a part of the deception. Considering years ago Eleanor had opened up to Anna about her and Franklin's past problems, Eleanor had thought she had Anna's support. Just a few years earlier Eleanor had written, "Today no one could ask for a better friend than I have in Anna, or she has in me… No one can tell either of us anything about the other; and though we might not always think alike or act alike, we always respect each other's motives, and there is a type of sympathetic understanding between us which would make a real misunderstanding quite impossible."[1]

Later in life, Elliot, Eleanor's son, remembers that Anna made light of the effects of this episode but truth be told, the strain between Anna and Eleanor lasted for years.[2] It only abates when Eleanor flew out to help Anna during a time of illness. Elliott records this insightful comment about the lack of support from the children for their mother. He says, "All of us made life hard for her. All of us failed her."[3]

A few months after the funeral, while Eleanor is going

through Franklin's possessions she comes across a water color that Lucy had commissioned of Franklin. Eleanor, as a gracious act, has it returned to Lucy.[4]

Franklin's casket is loaded on a railroad car and taken back to Washington. Eleanor rides on the train and for mile after mile she sees lines of people standing along the tracks to pay their respects. They had looked to Franklin, as sheep to a shepherd, to lead them out of the Depression and the war.

Eleanor respects what Franklin has given his people and will not impugn his character. That die had been cast back in 1918, and it isn't going to change even if Eleanor is now more outspoken. It is her choice to support the politically correct facade. It provides her a measure of privacy too. Any future reference to the inner conflicts of their relationship Eleanor refers to only with oblique comments.

She later relates of their relationship, "Perhaps it was much further back I had had to face certain difficulties until I decided to accept the fact that a man must be what he is, life must be lived as it is, circumstances force your children away from you, and you cannot live at all if you do not learn to adapt yourself to your life as it happens to be.

"All human beings have failings, all human beings have needs and temptations and stresses. Men and women who live together through long years get to know one another's failings; but they also come to know what is worthy of respect and admiration in those they live with and in themselves. If at the end one can say: "This man used to the limit the powers that God granted him; he was worthy of love and respect and of the sacrifices of many people, made in order that he might achieve what he deemed to be his task," then that life has been lived well and there are no regrets.

"He might have been happier with a wife who was completely uncritical. That I was never able to be, and he had to find it in some other people. Nevertheless, I think I sometimes acted as a spur, even though the spurring was not always wanted or welcome. I was one of those who served his purpose."[5]

Eleanor packs up her belongings from the White House and moves everything to Val-Kill. It is recorded that she turns to an inquisitive reporter and says, "The story is over."

Eleanor thinks she is retiring from public life. She is wrong. She just needs a time to collect herself. Her greatest gift to humanity is still ahead.

Part Three — Political, Public and Personal Storms
Reflections for the Reader

Who is our 'jingo' today? No chapter in history is complete without one.

⚡ Never wrestle with a pig. You both get dirty and the pig likes it.

The sniping of society is as predictable as a bar scene in a western.

Eleanor learns to pick her battles.

⚡ After slaying the dragon, the world is safe and the hero is on his way. Fiction stories end here.

Life doesn't.

⚡ A king's castle—a moat, protective high walls, guards in the watch towers. He is surrounded by people he can trust. He is safe to let down his guard, scratch his balls and drink grog with his cronies.

Eleanor's castle is Val-Kill.

Everyone needs a castle.

⚡ For the *Titanic*, the drama is the rippling effects of the crew deviating from their training not the crew being devious.

Eleanor was prepared for the mistakes of her inner circle and her children. Discovering the extent of shrewd desertion behind a façade of smiles was devastating.

The *Titanic* never recovered. Eleanor does.

PART FOUR
LIFE AFTER DEATH

FLASH

Context and Comments

You have a pretty good idea of what Eleanor contributed to the lives of people throughout the world. You have read lots of interesting stories and tidbits of information. You could stop now and just go on about your business, but there is more.

Her vision is expanding beyond civil rights for African Americans, far beyond equal pay for women, or building homes for the destitute. Eleanor will take time from these worthy causes because she comes to understand that if she can resolve the deeper issue—the other problems more readily solve themselves.

Eleanor's potential for dreaming big could have started when she was around her Uncle Teddy. For years he had envisioned parts of our country to be left as wilderness and set aside for 'the betterment and enjoyment of the people.' A National Park. No government in the world had done such a thing. And considering our country's collective mantra of 'subdue the wilderness,' setting aside land to stay wild is a radical concept. The idea gradually becomes reality, and the United States now has almost 400 parks enjoyed by 275 million visitors per year.

Is there anyone else Eleanor can look to as an example—where the goal is greater, the personal sacrifice more severe, and the brilliant vision is juxtaposed against a dark reality like lightening cracking against a storming sky?

Eleanor has a friend who for years has believed an outrageous idea. When their international schedules coincide, they meet for lunch. They share their dreams and pass ideas back and forth across the table like a salt shaker.

Eleanor knows this woman's life. She has risen above disillusionments that include the murder of millions, she has called out critics that are bullies armed with billions of dollars, and she has let go of stinging betrayals on an international scale. This woman, Golda Meir, doesn't quit.

As a child, Golda and her family leave Russia to escape the murderous anti-Semitism in Russia. They resettle in Milwaukee, Wisconsin. As a teenager, Golda alters her goal of raising money for her people back in Russia. She realizes that until Jews have their own nation with a government that defends its people, they will always be at the mercy of others. In her twenties, Golda joins the Zionist Movement and is one of the few Jews in the early 1900s who returns to the land her people had been forced to leave 2,000 years ago.

Every day Golda strives toward the dream of Israel becoming an independent nation in spite of the overwhelming facts to the contrary. She is living in a desert wasteland, raising chickens, washing clothes for other families and going hungry in order to feed her children.

The impossible circumstance for Golda's vision is not just the hostile people surrounding the land but this—there is not one nation in the world that will stand against the Arabs with their oil and help the Jews get some portion of land back.

Eleanor's dreams outsize both Teddy and Golda. Teddy wanted his people to have parks. In 1916 the National Park Service was created. Golda Meir wanted her people to have a place. She is a signer of their Declaration of Independence for the Nation State of Israel in 1948.

Eleanor wants people to have peace. This is a ridiculously impossible idea when considering that her generation has seen two world wars. For Eleanor, the magnitude of the circumstances is exactly the point.

12
PRAGMATIC PLANS FOR PEACE

In the life of any visionary person years are spent advocating for a change and continually educating the public. As far back as the 1920s Eleanor's mantra at every opportunity is, "The time to prepare for world peace is during the time of peace and not during the time of war."[1] Speaking at luncheons and dinner engagements, Eleanor faces one plate after another of chicken salad. It is grueling—not glamorous.

"Great minds discuss ideas, average minds discuss events, small minds discuss people"
Eleanor Roosevelt

After World War I, Eleanor is an activist in the organization 'World Foundation' with its purpose to promote U.S. entry to the World Court. A speech she gives in 1925 includes, "Now when many of the nations of the world are at peace and we still remember vividly the horrors of 1914-1918 and know fairly generally what the next war will mean, now is the time to act. Usually only the experts, technical people, busy with a war plan know, but at the moment we all know that the next war will be a war in which people not armies will suffer, and our boasted, hard earned civilization will do us no good."[2]

World War I—Trench Warfare

In 1933, still before WWII, she says, "We ought to be able to realize what people are up against in Europe. We ought to be the ready-to-understand ones, and we haven't been.... We've got to find a basis for a more stabilized world... We are in an ideal position to lead, if we will lead, because we have suffered less. Only a few years are left to work in. Everywhere over there is the dread of this war that may come."[3]

After WWI Eleanor sees the League of Nations and the emerging World Court as a tangible means for countries to work together and prevent a second world war. Franklin, in his first run for president, sees these two venues as political bargaining chips.

Randolph Hearst, American newspaper magnate, wants the U.S. to maintain an isolationist stand. He has promised Franklin the electoral votes of California and Texas in exchange for Franklin withholding United States membership to the World

Court and The League of Nations. When Eleanor learns of Franklin's convention promise, she is furious. Franklin gets the electoral votes, wins the presidency and the U.S. withholds its membership. In her disappointment and anger over this 'deal,' Eleanor doesn't speak to Franklin for days.[4]

"If we don't make this a more decent world to live in I don't see how we can look these boys in the eyes. They are going to fight their handicaps all their lives and what for if the world is the same cruel, stupid place."[5]
Eleanor Roosevelt, after her return from the Pacific, 1944

In her years of educating anyone who will listen, Eleanor, as First Lady, uses her position to discuss points that politicians and the media are loathe to expose: blind spots of the American psyche. Eleanor sees that in order to win a war, Americans always resolve to sacrifice their luxuries, give their resources and incur huge debt. She duly notes that Americans sees this as patriotic. In 1934 she extends a challenge to the DAR (Daughters of the American Revolution) to broaden their perspective and see that patriotism can also mean "living for the interests of everyone in our country and the world at large, rather than simply preparing to die for our country."[6]

Now in the midst of WWII, the inconsistency keeps its old grip. Citizens are willing to make sacrifices and buy war bonds. Children go door to door collecting used razor blades to be melted down for bombs. And yet the spirit of cooperation cannot extend to whites and blacks working together in factories. As the war rages in 1943, there are race riots in the U.S. In Detroit, 34 people are killed and Federal troops are called in to restore order after three days of rioting.

Bodies of U.S. officers and soldiers, killed after their capture by Nazi troops, Malmedy Belgium 12/11/1944

In reaction to this news, Eleanor writes in her "My Day" column, "… we cannot prepare for a peaceful world unless we give proof of self-restraint, of open mindedness, of courage to do right at home, even if it means changing our traditional thinking and, for some of us, a sacrifice of our material interests."[7]

After WWII, Eleanor is among the first to visit the concentration camps. She talks to Holocaust survivors who are refused traveling papers to go to Palestine (Israel has not yet been declared a nation) where Jews are prepared to provide for them. Instead, they are being held in detention centers alongside Nazi prisoners. In one instance, an elderly Jewish woman kneels at Eleanor's feet and cries out, "Israel, Israel." Eleanor finally understands, "for the first time what that small land meant to so many, many people."[8]

As Eleanor types the words for another article is she wondering if this suffering could have been avoided had the U.S. joined the League of Nations? In 1946 Eleanor writes the current circumstances, "clearly shows that we arrive at catastrophe by failing to meet situations—by failing to act where we should act... opportunity passes and the next situation always is more difficult than the last one."[9]

> *"More than ending war, we must put an end to the conditions that cause war."*
> *Eleanor Roosevelt*

Eleanor also visits a group of women in Stuttgart, Germany. She explains, "I had no intention of letting their coldness prevent me from saying certain things I had on my mind, so I began with a denunciation of the Nazi philosophy and actions. I made it as strong as I could, and I expressed the opinion that the German people must bear their share of the blame."[10]

To Eleanor's credit, she did not leave it there but goes on to acknowledge her appreciation to the people of Germany for assisting in the German Airlift efforts and helping defy Communist power. Her audience starts to soften, and she finishes her speech with this gracious offer, "And now I extend to you the hand of friendship and cooperation."[11]

After Franklin's death, Eleanor is encouraging President Truman to push the Democratic leadership to ensure that the final objective of World War II, plans for peace, is accomplished. Truman complains to her that the Democrats are tired. Eleanor responds, "Perhaps the people are too. Unfortunately, this is a bad time to be tired."[12]

In a radio broadcast from Paris, Eleanor reminds the listeners, "I think that what you want to know—especially you, the women of post-war Europe—is whether you shall be able, tomorrow, to tell your children that peace is at long last, a reality. For it isn't enough to talk about peace. One must believe in it. And it isn't enough to believe in it. One must work at it."[13]

Her pragmatic plan for peace includes tea. In 1960 Krushchev comes to the United States and speaks at the General Assembly of the U.N. It is the episode caught on film where he takes off his shoe and bangs it on his desk. Eleanor thinks Krushchev 'behaved outrageously.'[14] That doesn't keep her from inviting him to tea. When she is ridiculed for this act she responds, "We have to face the fact that either all of us are going to die together or we are going to learn to live together, and if we are to live together, we have to talk."[15]

Her perspective is a constant balance of working toward peace while believing the use of the atomic bomb was necessary. Faced with the argument that the U.S. was not justified in its use, Eleanor has this response, "I would like to review the circumstances which led up to this first use of the atomic bomb…"[16]

Eleanor reminds her readers, "Freedom makes a huge requirement of every human being. With freedom comes responsibility. For the person who is unwilling to grow up, the person who does not want to carry his own weight, this is a frightening prospect."

During Eleanor's years ahead, she too will continue to grow, learn and have her patience stretched.

13

UNITED NATIONS — AN OXYMORON

President Truman calls Eleanor. He is asking her to be one of the delegates to the newly formed United Nations.

The development of the U.N. has long had Eleanor's support. Its primary focus is maintaining international peace and to facilitate the cooperation between international communities in the areas of economic, social and humanitarian problems. Eleanor joins the United States Delegation to the United Nations General Assembly in December 1946.

First there is the back story.

The League of Nations was organized after World War I to prevent another world war. It failed.

The parts of the League's governing body that were successful are; the International Labor Organization, the International Court of Justice, and the World Health Organization. Commissions were set in place to tackle the problems of war refugees, slavery and protecting intellectual property rights.

The Labor Organization helped institute eight-hour-work-days, 48-hour-work weeks, keeping lead out of paint, ending child labor, and protecting women's rights in the workplace The Health Organization worked toward ending leprosy, malaria, yellow fever and preventing typhus epidemics.

These measures of success are remarkable considering that during the twenty-year-run of the League of Nations its members are never able to agree on even simple issues like a logo or flag. With differences in culture, philosophy, religion and government who on earth (literally) thinks the League members will agree on a world emblem let alone world issues. Germany quits. Japan and Italy get out. As previously explained, the United States never did join.

Staying aloof is not a solution. It is cowardly evasion. Eleanor Roosevelt

The subsequent international argument, World War II, finishes in 1945. The overwhelming fear that another world war will destroy the earth gives nations the will to try again.

This time it is called the United Nations and as a governing body, Eleanor is the spine. If she was serious about making plans for peace, now is the chance. It will take her undaunted faith in the human race to envision a Declaration of Human Rights. This effort will test her commitment and compassion because first she must get eighteen nations on her committee to come to a consensus.

"But leadership is a stern, demanding role and no person or state can lead without earning that right."

Eleanor's sense of urgency drives her to keep a grueling schedule in order to learn the international laws and review the briefing materials prepared by the State Department. The first assembly meets in London. Eleanor spends the long voyage across the ocean in preparation.

In her first press conference since leaving the White House, Eleanor acknowledges to reporters that the United Nations might not be "final and perfect," but "I think that if the atomic bomb did nothing more, it scared the people to the point where they realized that either they must do something about preventing war or there is a chance that there might be a morning when we would not wake up."[2]

Dealing with the male delegates will also take long hours of work. In letters to friends she voices her concern, "I knew that as the only woman on the delegation I was not very welcome."[3] and her assurance, "The delegation won't follow me, dear, but I think they won't like to propose anything they think I would not approve of!"[4]

In an opening ceremony that is to welcome the delegates to the General Assembly, Eleanor is a speaker and says, "We must be willing to learn the lesson that cooperation may imply compromise, but if it brings a world advance it is a gain for each individual nation. There will be those who doubt their ability to rise to these new heights, but the alternative is not possible to contemplate."[5]

The immediate goal of the U.N. is being taken seriously by the public. Eleanor overhears one woman as she leaves a meeting, "They must succeed, the future of the world depends on it."[6]

Being on the public stage again makes her the object of criticism. Westbrook Pegler (from earlier chapters) decries how much Eleanor will be paid. He says Eleanor has been given, "a political job paying $12,000 a year, which is $2,000 more than the salary of a Senator or Representative" He doesn't mention that Eleanor has refused the lifetime yearly pension of $5,000 that Congress had voted to allow widows of presidents.

Eleanor is assigned to Committee III. Her fellow delegates,  want to keep her in the back waters where there will be no opportunity for controversy, she'll have the least influence and she will not be in the way. Eleanor is to be President and Chair of the United Nations Commission on Human Rights. Its purpose is to deal with humanitarian, social and cultural matters.

Eleanor speaking at the United Nations

Although the membership to this group involves 18 countries, Eleanor with her usual aplomb, is determined to accomplish the Declaration of Human Rights as an international standard by which to hold countries accountable. Much like the Declaration of Independence is quoted in courts giving maligned citizens the tangible proof of disconnect between their situation and an agreed upon written word, Eleanor wants to give people throughout the world the same viable leverage.

Building a consensus in this diverse committee proves difficult. Eleanor finds she has much to learn even in the realm of women's rights. New circumstances force her to see her own blind spots and then reevaluate and define her opinions.

Eleanor is confronted by ladies who want the declaration to include the word 'women.' Eleanor believes that other countries will see

"In our thinking about them we must remember how the situation looks from their point of view."[7]

the word 'men' as being inclusive of women too. She recognizes she is thinking from an idealistic perspective. In other countries if the word 'men' is used in a document then it will only apply to men. Eleanor agrees with the wording of "All people are born equal" rather than "all men."[8]

Eleanor will continue to reexamine her decisions to give direct support to women's issues. Two women representing the World Women's Party for Equal Rights request Eleanor to give them her support. Although Eleanor agrees there should be more women delegates, she defers from giving them her direct support. Eleanor's goal is for women to be represented in an increased number of delegates, not special delegates.

When negotiating with the Soviet Union, her initial efforts are to make concessions. She sees this as a good faith measure. Realizing this doesn't work, she changes gear, and then, publicly states she will not compromise, "even on words. The Soviets look on this as evidence of weakness rather than as a gesture of good will."[9]

Her amended maneuvering leads to this comment by a State Department advisor; "Never have I seen naiveté and cunning so gracefully blended," This could be in reference to the new Eleanor who starts a rebuttal to a debate with the Communists by saying, "Now, of course, I'm a woman and don't understand all these things,…."[10]

In the midst of this the Russians also change their strategy. Initially they treat Eleanor as the widow of President Roosevelt and regard her with dismissive respect. When they realize she is a force to be reckoned with the Russians then characterize her as a "hypocritical servant of capitalism… a fly darkening the Soviet sun."[11] The Russian delegate Andrei Vishinsky considers her a meddling old woman.

For the contents of the human rights declaration, there are two opposing views. The United States and her allies want a document similar to the Declaration of Independence and the Bill of Rights. The Soviets don't want an emphasis on freedom of speech and fair trials but a declaration that stresses economic and social rights.

It is difficult for the U.S. to argue from the point of any moral high ground when within its own borders there is disregard for the rights of African Americans and high regard to not offend white southern voters. This weakens the U.S. stand and gives the Russian delegates a trump card to play.

Case in point, Dr. W.E.B. Du Bois through the NAACP has placed a petition against the United States to the United Nations. Russia suggests sending a team of theirs to investigate the NAACP petition. Eleanor knows she must agree and yet she must block their move. She counters with her own offer. She suggests sending a U.S. team to investigate the complaints coming from Russia. Russia backs down.

Coinciding with the case, Walter White (he sent Eleanor the Claude Neal lynching report) asks Eleanor to take part in a demonstration. Eleanor declines on grounds of compromising her position as a U.N. delegate. Her discretion proves helpful in getting the Russians to drop the NAACP case, but leverage for civil rights in the United States is sacrificed.

The Human Rights Committee has ended up being anything but backwaters for Eleanor. Instead, they are having high profile debates on how to handle the war refugees. Communist Russia and their eastern bloc countries insist the refugees should return or stay in their country of origin. Many of the refugees do not want to go back to their country of origin because that government has changed. This also relates to the Jewish refugees that Eleanor had seen after World War II. They are still being kept in Germany. Russia is expecting Jews to stay in a country that had a national policy to exterminate them.

Eleanor's days of being a doormat are decades behind her. Her fluency in French gives her negotiating an extra advantage. Over the months she has become an accomplished diplomat who holds a gavel. In this instance, as Chairman of the Human Rights Commission, she has been listening to a ranting delegate long enough. She relates, "I watched him closely until he had to pause for a breath. Then I banged the gavel so hard that the other delegates jumped in surprise and, before he could continue, I got in a few words of my own. "We are here," I said, "to devise ways of safeguarding human rights. We are not here to attack each other's governments, and I hope when we return on Monday the delegate of the Soviet Union will remember that!" I banged the gavel again. "Meeting adjourned!"[12]

By now Eleanor is garnering the respect of her fellow delegates. John Foster Dulles and Senator Vandenberg tell Eleanor, "Mrs. Roosevelt we must tell you that we did all we could to keep you off the United Nations delegation. We begged the President not to nominate you. But now we feel we must acknowledge that we have worked with you gladly and found you good to work with. And we will be happy to do so again."[13] Senator Vandenberg also says at a dinner, "I want to say that I take back everything I ever said about her, and believe me it's been plenty."[14]

Eleanor will even manage to change the perspective of the U.N. Russian delegate. Years later there is a public fund raising party for Eleanor's seventieth birthday and Mr. Vishinsky attends. This action is noteworthy because the monies raised are going to support the American Association for the U.N., which is the last thing one would have expected Mr. Vishinsky to support. At this event he recognizes he will not be seated with Eleanor's friends but says he will be, "very glad to sit anywhere."[15]

Wording for the Universal Declaration of Human Rights is finally hammered out and it is on the agenda of the Committee III. It will be up for vote.

Not so fast.

"Unless we can divest ourselves of that self-righteous feeling of superiority we are going to find it hard to understand how other people feel about their people, their history, their heroes and achievements."[16]

**Eleanor Roosevelt
at United Nations in Paris, 1951**

The Committee decides it is still up for debate and devotes 85 meetings to discussing the Declaration. It is certainly a detour for Eleanor's stride, but she is not deterred. The Soviets continue to delay and postpone, but eventually all objections are ironed out. The process has taken twenty-three months.

December 10, 1948 the Universal Declaration of Human Rights is adopted by the General Assembly. In recognition of Eleanor's leadership in this work she is given a standing ovation.

To this date, the declaration continues to be a binding document as law for many nations. But its power is still slow and limited.

September 2010, there was a news release that the United Nations was finally admitting it had failed to prevent the systematic gang rape of over 500 hundred women in the Democratic Republic of Congo this summer. Atul Khare, a senior official in the U.N. says, "Our actions were not adequate, resulting in the unacceptable brutalization of the population of the villages in the area. We must do better."

U.N. peacekeeping troops had been just 10 miles away.

**Eleanor Roosevelt and United Nations Universal
Declaration of Human Rights in Spanish text, 1949**

14
ELANOR

The chapter title is not a typo.

Eleanor has retired from her work at the U.N. She has transcended being an American and has become an ambassador of good will to the world. People of all nationalities love her and newspaper headlines read, "First Lady of the World."

Ambassador Lewis Douglas reports from London "Everywhere she went large crowds greeted her enthusiastically."[1] A Swedish newspaper notes, "She did not try to impress us, she did impress us."[2] Sir Benegal Rau, from India refers to her as, "an American phenomenon comparable to the Niagara Falls."[3]

On her trip to Pakistan and India (age 68) she gives speeches about the League of Woman Voters. That is not amazing. Nor is it surprising as she arrives at New Delhi she states, "I have come here to learn."[4] What is the poignant reminder of human kindness without airs is a photo of her amidst a group of young women. Eleanor is teaching them a dance, the Virginia Reel.[5]

Quickly shifting gears to give polished diplomatic responses, Eleanor includes poise and wit. She visits Russia and has an interview with Khrushchev. When she is leaving he asks her, "Can I tell our papers that we have had a friendly conversation?" Eleanor replies, "You can say that we had a friendly conversation but that we differ." Khrushchev laughs and answers, "Now, we didn't shoot at each other."[6]

An organizer of an event is worried the audience will boo Eleanor. Eleanor responds, "Don't worry about it. I have been booed for 15 minutes at a time—it doesn't bother me."[7]

Her thick FBI file doesn't make her wince either. In fact, she thrives on a good fight. "After all these years, I've learned not to let that sort of thing get me down."[8] And now instead of hiding from her critics she says, "If I could be worried about mud-slinging, I would have been dead long ago…"[9] She also adds, "Curiously enough it is often the people who refuse to assume any responsibility who are apt to be the sharpest critics of those who do."[10]

A continued great pleasure for Eleanor is using her years of connections and contacts to bring direct help and solve a problem. In 1956 Eleanor is made aware of the plight of ten thousand Jews who had reached Casablanca, but now were prevented from leaving for Israel. Eleanor had just received the ambassador of Morocco, who had expressed his gratitude to Eleanor for Franklin's help to his country. Eleanor writes a request to the sultan of Morocco and a few days later the Jew are released to go to Israel.[11]

It is sixteen years after Franklin's death, and Eleanor continues to be voted the "Most Admired Woman" in America. This precludes Jacqueline Kennedy, Queen Elizabeth, Mrs. Dwight Eisenhower, and Mme. Chaing Kai-shek.[12]

During an interview Eleanor is asked about her self-confidence and if she has always been this way. Eleanor responds, "No. When I was young I was very self-conscious."

Then she is asked, "How did you overcome this?"

Eleanor answers, "Little by little. As life developed, I faced each problem as it came along. As my activities and work broadened and reached out, I never tried to shirk. I tried never to evade an issue. When I found I had something to do—I just did it…"[13]

"I would like to see us take hold of ourselves, look at ourselves and cease being afraid."[14]
Eleanor at her 70th birthday party

Eleanor's optimism glosses over some parts of her life where an attitude of 'just do it' just didn't work. This applies to her children who are now adults with families of their own.

From their beginnings with the benevolent grandmother and knowing their father is either Governor of New York or President of the United States, it is understandable the lives of Anna, James, Elliott, Franklin Jr., and John being skewed. Amongst them they will total fifteen divorces.

In numerous correspondences Eleanor blames herself for her children's shortfalls. She writes to Hick, "I don't seem to be able to shake the feeling of responsibility for Elliott and Anna. I guess I was a pretty unwise teacher as to how to go about living. Too late to do anything now, however, and I'm rather disgusted with myself. I feel soiled, ..."[15]

Eleanor with her demanding schedule is often in a swirling mode of guilt and in her later years tries to make up for her lacks, whether real or imagined, in motherhood. In order to be with her children during illness and the birth of babies, Eleanor cancels trips and speaking engagements. She assumes Sara's role of financial indulgences, justifying monetary gifts with excuses of the children's struggles being her fault.

To assist her children, Eleanor will use the draw of her name to help them with business ventures. She has a radio talk show with her daughter Anna. With Elliott she is the television host attracting big names such as Albert Einstein.

Happiness is not a goal; it is a by-product.
Eleanor saying

When the children are all home for a holiday, which includes spouses and kids, dinner discussions can degrade to an angry bout with no one holding back sarcastic barbs. The quarreling, the divorces, and the unhappiness in her children's lives reverts Eleanor to her old days of depression, which she calls her "Griselda mood." Unable to find a way to help, because it is ultimately up to the other person, Eleanor isolates herself and at times takes to her bed.

When she is told that her former son-in-law has committed suicide, Eleanor is in despair. To her doctor, an intimate friend she relays, "My children would be much better off if I were not alive. I'm overshadowing them."[16]

Eleanor Roosevelt and John F. Kennedy, 1961

Throughout the fifties Eleanor continues to give over one hundred and fifty speeches each year. She feels she is needed and she will not slow down. At the request of President John F. Kennedy she takes the job as Chair of the Presidential Commission on the Status of Women and the National Advisory Committee of the Peace Corps.

She dines with Marshal Tito, the Prime Minister of Yugoslavia, greets Prime Minister Nehru of India, advises President Truman, meets with her old friend Churchill or chats with Golda Meir the future Prime Minister of Israel. When she is home at Val-Kill she takes time to show children's groups through Springwood which has become a national historic site. She invites a group from a boys' home for African American children to come visit every summer for a picnic.

Until the end, Eleanor is always busy living her life. Hers is a good example of a quote by Don Quixote she would often use, "Until death it is all life."[17]

Eleanor later writes, "On that seventy-fifth birthday I knew I had long since become aware of my over-all objective in life. It stemmed from those early impressions I had gathered when I saw war-torn Europe after World War I. I wanted, with all my heart, a peaceful world. And I knew it could never be achieved on a lasting basis without greater understanding between peoples. It is to these ends that I have, in the main, devoted the past years."[18]

The inner drive to never disappoint is still strong even at the age of 78. In 1962 after a long day of meeting and greeting she still has one more stop. Eleanor's aide recommends she cancel. Eleanor does acknowledge that "My head is heavy and if I go, you'll have to steady me when I get out of the car." While Eleanor greets the crowd, a young African American girl steps forward to give her an armful of flowers. Eleanor responds to the aide, "You see I had to come. I was expected."[19]

In the last years of her life, Eleanor suffers from aplastic anemia (bone-marrow failure). She had been brought home and in typical gracious fashion she tells her assistant, "Maureen, I forgot to thank the stretcher-bearers. Will you please tell them that I think they did a magnificent job."[20]

During the final months, does she look out at the pool and linger with memories of her grandchildren or dignitaries splashing about? Does she recall the aroma of hotdogs being grilled by Franklin as he sat in his wheelchair?

Wandering through the rooms of her home does she have a knowing look of pleasure seeing them devoid of ostentatious diplomatic gifts? Does she pause and adjust one of the hundred framed photos, all of family and friends, she has hung on the walls?

Sitting at her desk is there a ghostly ache in her wrist for the days she kept signing her name? Does she reach over and straighten her name plate, remembering the young student who had made it for her in shop class? Is the purpose of keeping this at the front of her desk, to be a message for any visiting dignitary to walk humbly? The young man had carved her name, "Elanor."

It's still on Eleanor's desk at Val-Kill today.

Her influence was international and yet she never forgot to be a human being of consequence. In the opening of her book, *You Learn by Living*, she reminds us, "In the long run, we shape our lives, and we shape ourselves. The process never ends until we die. And the choices we make are ultimately our own responsibility."

She died November 7, 1962.

Part Four   Life After Death
Reflections for the Reader

"Space: the final frontier. These are the voyages of the starship *Enterprise*. Its five-year mission: to explore strange new worlds, to seek out new life and new civilizations, to boldly go where no man has gone before." Captain Kirk, USS *Enterprise*.

Peace: the highest goal. These are the journeys of a woman, code name *Rover*. She traveled thousands of miles over land, sea and air to listen and learn from other civilizations. Her calm assurance, never deterring from the destiny of peace, made her the world renowned Ambassador of Peace.

Dorothy is brushing off her red shoes. She just got a call from Glinda the good witch. There's trouble back in Oz, and they need her.

Eleanor gets called back to action. She is wise, gracious and still open to her own learning. Plus, she loves the challenge.

There are no exciting movies about the long years of building the Wall of China. Stirring mud and straw to make bricks is not interesting unless there is an attack by Genghis Kahn.

Eleanor spends years, working within an imperfect group, building toward a vision of peace in the world. The Universal Declaration of Human Rights was her Wall of China.

Everyone has a journey. Moses, Odysseus, Pocahontas, Huck Finn, Mr. Smith, Pip, Dorothy and Toto, Harry Potter, Laurence of Arabia, John Adams, Benjamin Franklin, Harriet Tubman, Golda Meir, Eleanor and you.

No one, truth or fiction, is ever given a map. Your journey simply starts with the first step.

BIBLIOGRAPHY

Adams, Henry: *The Education of Henry Adams,* ed. Ernest Samuels (Boston, 1973; orig. pub. 1907).

Brands, H.W.: *Traitor to His Class: The Privileged Life and Radical Presidency of Franklin Delano Roosevelt* (Anchor Books 2008).

Cohen, Robert: *Dear Mrs. Roosevelt: Letters from Children of the Great Depression,* (The University of North Carolina Press 2002).

Cook, Blanche Wiesen: *Eleanor Roosevelt Volume 1 1884-1933,* (Viking Penguin 1992).
  Eleanor Roosevelt Volume 2 The Defining Years 1933-1938, (Viking Penguin 1999).

Dray, Philip: *At the Hands Of Persons Unknown,* (Modern Library 2002)

Gerber, Robin: *Leadership the Eleanor Roosevelt Way: Timeless Strategies from the First Lady of Courage,* (Penguin Books 2002).

Goodwin, Doris Kearns: *No Ordinary Time: Franklin and Eleanor Roosevelt: The Home Front in World War II,* (Simon &Schuster 1994).

Kaledin, Eugenia: *The Education of Mrs. Henry Adams,* (University of Massachusetts Press Amherst, 1981)

Lash, Joseph P.: *Eleanor: The Years Alone,* (W W Norton & Company Inc 1972)
  Eleanor And Franklin, (W W Norton & Company Inc 1971).
  A World of Love, (Doubleday & Company, Inc. 1984).

Miller, Kristie and McGinnis, Robert H.: *The Letters of*

Eleanor Roosevelt and Isabella Greenway 1904-1953, (The Arizona Historical Society 2009).

Roosevelt, Eleanor: *My Day: The Best of Eleanor Roosevelt's Acclaimed Newspaper Columns, 1936-1962*, (Da Capo Press 2001).
    Tomorrow is Now, (Harper & Row, Publishers 1963).
    You Learn By Living, (The Westminster Press 1960).
    The Autobiography of Eleanor Roosevelt, (Da Capo Press 1992).

Roosevelt, Elliott & Brough, James: *Mother R.: Eleanor Roosevelt's Untold Story* (G.P. Putnam's Sons 1977).
    The Roosevelts of Hyde Park: An Untold Story (G.P. Putnam's Sons 1973).

Showalter, Elaine: *A Jury of Her Peers* (Vintage Books 2009).

Smith, Jean Edward: *FDR,* (Random House Trade Paperbacks 2007).

ENDNOTES
Part One — A Bitter Beginning

Context and Commentary

_____

[1] *Child Abuse: History, Laws and the A.S.P.C.A.* by Darlene Barriere SelfGrowth.com

Chapter One — Childhood

[2] Cook, E*leanor Roosevelt, Volume 1, 1884 - 1933*, 1992 — p. 35, 37.

[3] Ibid., p. 43.

[4] Lash J. P., *Eleanor and Franklin*, 1971 — p. 24.

[5] Ibid., p. 33.

[6] Goodwin, 1994 — p. 93.

[7] Roosevelt, *The Autobiography of Eleanor Roosevelt*, 1992 — p. 7.

[8] Cook, *Eleanor Roosevelt, Volume 1, 1884 - 1933*, 1992 — p. 67.

[9] Ibid. p. 78.

[10] Ibid, p. 86.

[11] Lash J. P., *Eleanor and Franklin,* 1971 — p. 55.

[12] Ibid. p. 56

[13] Cook, *Eleanor Roosevelt, Volume 1, 1884 - 1933*, 1992 — p. 82

[14] Lash J.P., *Eleanor and Franklin,* 1971 — p. 198

[15] Ibid. p. 61.

[16] Ibid. p. 61.

Chapter Two — Adolescence

[1] Brands, 2008, p. 37

[2] Cook, *Eleanor Roosevelt, Volume 1, 1884 - 1933*, 1992 — p. 107.

[3] Ibid. p. 369.

[4] Ibid. p. 110.

[5] Ibid. p. 121.

[6] Roosevelt, *The Autobiography of Eleanor Roosevelt*, 1992 — p. 37.

[7] Cook, *Eleanor Roosevelt, Volume 1, 1884 - 1933*, 1992 — p. 130.

[8] Roosevelt, *The Autobiography of Eleanor Roosevelt*, 1992 — p. 40.

Chapter Three — Marriage

[1] Cook, *Eleanor Roosevelt, Volume 1, 1884 - 1933*, 1992 — p. 146.

[2] Lash J. P., *Eleanor and Franklin*, 1971 — p. 113.

[3] Ibid. p. 113.

[4] Cook, *Eleanor Roosevelt, Volume 1, 1884 - 1933*, 1992 — p. 144.

[5] Goodwin, 1994 — p. 275.

[6] Cook, *Eleanor Roosevelt, Volume 1, 1884 - 1933*, 1992 — p. 157.

[7] Lash J. P., *Eleanor and Franklin*, 1971 — p. 121.

[8] Cook, *Eleanor Roosevelt, Volume 1, 1884 - 1933*, 1992 — p. 158.

[9] Lash J. P., *Eleanor and Franklin*, 1971 — p. 136.

[10] Cook, *Eleanor Roosevelt, Volume 1, 1884 - 1933*, 1992 — p. 154.

[11] Ibid. p. 172.

[12] Ibid. p. 174.

[13] Smith, 2007 — p. 55.

[14] Roosevelt, *The Autobiography of Eleanor Roosevelt*, 1992 — p. 66.

[15] Goodwin, 1994 — p. 179.

[16] Brough E. R., 1977 — p. 56.

[17] Goodwin, 1994 — p. 179.

[18] Roosevelt, *My Day, the Best of Eleanor Roosevelt's Acclaimed Newspaper Columns*, 1936-1962, 2001 — p. 29.

[19] Lash J. P., *Eleanor and Franklin*, 1971 — p. 242.

[20] Ibid. p. 243.

[21] Ibid. p. 278.

[22] Ibid. p. 276.

[23] Ibid. p. 220.

Chapter Four — Crisis

[1] Cook, *Eleanor Roosevelt, Volume 1, 1884 - 1933*, 1992 — p. 215.

[2] Goodwin, 1994 — p. 453.

[3] Cook, *Eleanor Roosevelt, Volume 1, 1884 - 1933*, 1992 — p. 218.

[4] Roosevelt, *The Autobiography of Eleanor Roosevelt*, 1992 — p. 412.

Part Two — Awakening
Chapter Five — Emancipation

[1] Kaledin, 1981 — p. 3.

[2] Lash J. P., *Eleanor and Franklin,* 1971 — p. 237.

[3] Lash J. P., *Eleanor: The Years Alone,* 1972 — p. 238.

[4] Lash J. P., *Eleanor and Franklin,* 1971 — p. 276.

[5] Cook, *Eleanor Roosevelt, Volume 1, 1884 - 1933,* 1992 — p. 363.

[6] Lash J. P., *Eleanor and Franklin,* 1971 — p. 287.

[7] Lash J. P., *Eleanor: The Years Alone,* 1972 — p. 168.

[8] Cook, *Eleanor Roosevelt, Volume 1, 1884 - 1933,* 1992 — p. 257.

Chapter Six — Compassion

[1] Goodwin, 1994 — p. 90.

[2] Lash J. P., *Eleanor and Franklin,* 1971 — p. 350

[3] Cook, *Eleanor Roosevelt, Volume 2, The Defining Years, 1933 - 1938,* 1999 — p. 13.

[4] Lash J. P., *Eleanor and Franklin,* 1971 — p. 374.

[5] Ibid. p. 374

[6] Cook, *Eleanor Roosevelt, Volume 2, The Defining Years, 1933 - 1938,* 1999 — p. 50.

[7] Ibid. p. 32.

[8] Lash J. P., *Eleanor and Franklin,* 1971 — p. 372.

[9] Ibid. p. 374.

[10] Cook, *Eleanor Roosevelt, Volume 2, The Defining Years, 1933 - 1938,* 1999 — p. 24.

[11] Roosevelt, *The Autobiography of Eleanor Roosevelt,* 1992 — p. 109.

[12] Lash J. P., *Eleanor and Franklin,* 1971 — p. 363.

[13] Cook, *Eleanor Roosevelt, Volume 2, The Defining Years, 1933 - 1938,* 1999 — p. 329.

[14] Lash J. P., *Eleanor and Franklin,* 1971 — p. 392.

[15] Ibid. p. 392.

[16] Ibid. p. 455.

[17] Cook, *Eleanor Roosevelt, Volume 2, The Defining Years, 1933 - 1938,*

1999 — p. 32.

[18] Ibid. p. 347.

[19] Ibid. p. 347.

[20] Ibid. p. 93.

[21] Ibid. p. 349.

[22] Roosevelt, *My Day, the Best of Eleanor Roosevelt's Acclaimed Newspaper Columns,* 1936-1962, 2001 — p. 37.

[23] Lash J. P., *Eleanor: The Years Alone,* 1972 — p. 304.

[24] Ibid. p. 305.

[25] Lash J. P., *Eleanor and Franklin,* 1971 — p. 392.

[26] Roosevelt, *You Learn By Living,* 1960 — p. 107.

[27] Cook, *Eleanor Roosevelt, Volume 2, The Defining Years, 1933 - 1938,* 1999 — p. 142.

[28] Ibid. p. 137.

[29] Cook, *Eleanor Roosevelt, Volume 2, The Defining Years, 1933 - 1938,* 1999 — p. 331.

[30] Ibid. p. 249.

[31] Ibid. p. 148.

[32] Ibid. p. 65.

[33] Ibid. p. 422.

[34] Ibid. p. 268.

[35] Ibid. p. 152.

Chapter Seven — Causes

[1] Dray, 2003 — p. 82.

[2] Goodwin, 1994 — p. 446

[3] Lash J. P., *Eleanor: The Years Alone,* 1972 — p. 255

[4] Lash J. P., *Eleanor and Franklin,* 1971 — p. 238

[5] Cook, *Eleanor Roosevelt, Volume 2, The Defining Years, 1933 - 1938,* 1999 — p. 439

[6] Cook, *Eleanor Roosevelt, Volume 1, 1884 - 1933,* 1992 — p. 252

[7] Cook, *Eleanor Roosevelt, Volume 2, The Defining Years, 1933 - 1938,* 1999 — p. 159

[8] Roosevelt, *You Learn By Living,* 1960 — p. 186.

[9] Cook, *Eleanor Roosevelt, Volume 2, The Defining Years, 1933 - 1938,* 1999 — p. 243

[10] Ibid. p. 185

[11] Ibid. p. 185

[12] Ibid. p. 186

[13] Cook, *Eleanor Roosevelt, Volume 2, The Defining Years, 1933 - 1938,* 1999 — p. 185

[14] Goodwin, 1994 — p. 328

[15] Ibid. p. 328

[16] Goodwin, 1994 — p. 627

[17] Lash J. P., *Eleanor: The Years Alone,* 1972 — p. 691

[18] Cook, *Eleanor Roosevelt, Volume 2, The Defining Years, 1933 - 1938,* 1999 — p. 441

[19] Ibid. p. 128

[20] Ibid. p. 100

[21] Goodwin, 1994 — p. 447

[22] Roosevelt, *My Day, the Best of Eleanor Roosevelt's Acclaimed Newspaper Columns,* 1936-1962, 2001 — p. 305

[23] Goodwin, 1994 — p. 172

[24] Lash J. P., *Eleanor: The Years Alone,* 1972 — p. 310

[25] Cook, *Eleanor Roosevelt, Volume 2, The Defining Years, 1933 - 1938,* 1999 — p. 155

[26] Ibid. p. 565

[27] Ibid. p. 292

[28] Ibid. p. 440

[29] Goodwin, 1994 — p. 446

[30] (Lash J. P., *Eleanor and Franklin,* 1971 — p. 526

[31] Roosevelt, *My Day, the Best of Eleanor Roosevelt's Acclaimed Newspaper Columns,* 1936-1962, 2001 — p. 190

[32] Roosevelt, *My Day, the Best of Eleanor Roosevelt's Acclaimed Newspaper Columns,* 1936-1962, 2001 — p. 274

[33] Ibid. p. 231

[34] Ibid. p. 231

[35] Ibid. p. 162

[36] Goodwin, 1994 — p. 206

[37] Cook, *Eleanor Roosevelt, Volume 1, 1884 - 1933*, 1992 — p. 195

[38] Ibid. p. 200

[39] Ibid. p. 369

[40] Cook, *Eleanor Roosevelt, Volume 2, The Defining Years, 1933 - 1938*, 1999 — p. 284

[41] Ibid. p. 62

[42] Cook, *Eleanor Roosevelt, Volume 1, 1884 - 1933*, 1992 — p. 468

[43] Cook, *Eleanor Roosevelt, Volume 2, The Defining Years, 1933 - 1938*, 1999 — p. 77

[44] Ibid. p. 70

[45] Ibid. p. 73

[46] Ibid. p. 103

[47] Lash J. P., *Eleanor and Franklin*, 1971 — p. 288

[48] Lash J. P., *Eleanor: The Years Alone*, 1972 — p. 217

[49] Lash J. P., *Eleanor: The Years Alone*, 1972 — p. 54

[50] Cook, *Eleanor Roosevelt, Volume 1, 1884 - 1933*, 1992 — p. 390

[51] Cook, *Eleanor Roosevelt, Volume 2, The Defining Years, 1933 - 1938*, 1999 — p. 318

[52] Ibid. p. 128

[53] Lash J. P., *Eleanor and Franklin*, 1971 — p. 575

[54] Cook, *Eleanor Roosevelt, Volume 2, The Defining Years, 1933 - 1938*, 1999 — p. 304

[55] Ibid. p. 557

[56] Cook, *Eleanor Roosevelt, Volume 2, The Defining Years, 1933 - 1938*, 1999 — p. 571

[57] Lash J. P., *Eleanor: The Years Alone*, 1972 — p. 120

[58] Ibid. p. 121

[59] Ibid. p. 116

Chapter Eight — War

[1] Roosevelt, *You Learn By Living*, 1960 — p. 30-31

[2] Lash J. P., *Eleanor and Franklin*, 1971 — p. 579

[3] Goodwin, 1994 — p. 84

4 Lash J. P., *Eleanor and Franklin,* 1971 — p. 584

5 Ibid. p. 556

6 Cook, *Eleanor Roosevelt, Volume 2, The Defining Years, 1933 - 1938,* 1999 — p. 452

7 Lash J. P., *Eleanor and Franklin,* 1971 — p. 687

8 Roosevelt, *The Autobiography of Eleanor Roosevelt,* 1992 — p. 155

9 Lash J. P., *Eleanor and Franklin,* 1971 — p. 685

10 Ibid. p. 691

11 Roosevelt, *The Autobiography of Eleanor Roosevelt,* 1992 — p. 259

12 Roosevelt, *My Day, the Best of Eleanor Roosevelt's Acclaimed Newspaper Columns,* 1936-1962, 2001 — p. 103

13 Ibid. p. 104

14 Ibid. p. 105

15 Ibid. p. 103

Part Three — Political and Personal Storms
Chapter Nine — Critics

1 Showalter, *A Jury of Her Peers,* 2009 — p. 312

2 Ibid. p. 332

3 Ibid. p. 333

4 Showalter, *A Jury of Her Peers,* 2009 — p. 211

5 Lash J. P., *Eleanor and Franklin,* 1971 — p. 470

6 Roosevelt, *My Day, the Best of Eleanor Roosevelt's Acclaimed Newspaper Columns,* 1936-1962, 2001 — p. 184

7 Lash J. P., *Eleanor: The Years Alone,* 1972 — p. 234

8 Ibid. p. 235

9 Cook, *Eleanor Roosevelt, Volume 1, 1884 - 1933,* 1992 — p. 19

10 Ibid. p. 15

11 Lash J. P., *Eleanor: The Years Alone,* 1972 — p. 235

12 Ibid. p. 111

13 Eleanor Roosevelt. (n.d.). Great-Quotes.com. Retrieved December 9, 2011, from Great-Quotes.com Web site: http://www.great-quotes.com/quote/939575

14 Lash J. P., *Eleanor and Franklin,* 1971 — p. 389

[15] Cook, *Eleanor Roosevelt, Volume 1, 1884 - 1933*, 1992 — p. 304

[16] Lash J. P., *Eleanor and Franklin*, 1971 — p. 391

[17] Cook, *Eleanor Roosevelt, Volume 2, The Defining Years, 1933 - 1938*, 1999 — p. 484

[18] Ibid. p. 552

[19] Cook, *Eleanor Roosevelt, Volume 1, 1884 - 1933*, 1992 — p. 499

[20] Ibid. p. 499

[21] Lash J. P., *Eleanor and Franklin*, 1971 — p. 349

[22] Roosevelt, *The Autobiography of Eleanor Roosevelt*, 1992 — p. 245

[23] Lash J. P., *Eleanor and Franklin*, 1971 — p. 668

[24] Goodwin, 1994 — p. 457

Chapter Ten — Refuge

[1] Lash J. P., *Eleanor and Franklin*, 1971 — p. 506

[2] Lash J. P., *Eleanor and Franklin*, 1971 — p. 492

[3] Ibid. p. 492

[4] Ibid. p. 492

[5] Cook, *Eleanor Roosevelt, Volume 2, The Defining Years, 1933 - 1938*, 1999 — p. 95

[6] Ibid. p. 94

[7] Lash J. P., *Eleanor and Franklin*, 1971 — p. 421

[8] Cook, *Eleanor Roosevelt, Volume 2, The Defining Years, 1933 - 1938*, 1999 — p. 96

[9] Ibid. p. 253

[10] Ibid. p. 206

[11] Lash J.P., *Eleanor and Franklin*, 1971 — p. 679

[12] Ibid. p. 111

[13] Cook, *Eleanor Roosevelt, Volume 2, The Defining Years, 1933 - 1938*, 1999 — p. 260

[14] Roosevelt, *You Learn By Living*, 1960 — p. 26

[15] Cook, *Eleanor Roosevelt, Volume 1, 1884 - 1933*, 1992 — p. 435

[16] Cook, *Eleanor Roosevelt, Volume 2, The Defining Years, 1933 - 1938*, 1999 — p. 58

[17] Ibid. p. 525

Chapter Eleven — Blindsided by Family

[1] Brough E. R., 1973 — p. 168

[2] Brough E. R., 1977 — p. 31

[3] Lash J. P., *Eleanor: The Years Alone*, 1972 — p. 181

[4] Goodwin, 1994 — p. 630

[5] Lash J. P., *Eleanor and Franklin*, 1971 — p. 722

Part Four — Life After Death
Chapter Twelve — Pragmatic Plans for Peace

[1] Cook, *Eleanor Roosevelt, Volume 1, 1884 - 1933*, 1992 — p. 365

[2] Lash J. P., *Eleanor and Franklin*, 1971 — p. 286

[3] Ibid. p. 363

[4] Cook, *Eleanor Roosevelt, Volume 2, The Defining Years, 1933 - 1938*, 1999 — p. 99

[5] Lash J. P., *Eleanor and Franklin*, 1971 — p. 692

[6] Ibid. p. 420

[7] Roosevelt, *My Day, the Best of Eleanor Roosevelt's Acclaimed Newspaper Columns*, 1936-1962, 2001 — p. 80

[8] Lash J. P., *Eleanor: The Years Alone*, 1972 — p. 116

[9] Cook, *Eleanor Roosevelt, Volume 1, 1884 - 1933*, 1992 — p. 17

[10] Roosevelt, *The Autobiography of Eleanor Roosevelt*, 1992 — p. 321

[11] Ibid. p. 321

[12] Lash J. P., *Eleanor: The Years Alone*, 1972 — p. 145

[13] Ibid. p. 196

[14] Ibid. p. 273

[15] Ibid. p. 273

[16] Roosevelt, *My Day, the Best of Eleanor Roosevelt's Acclaimed Newspaper Columns*, 1936-1962, 2001 — p. 235

Chapter Thirteen — United Nations an Oxymoron

[1] Roosevelt, *The Autobiography of Eleanor Roosevelt*, 1992 — p. 368

[2] Lash J. P., *Eleanor: The Years Alone*, 1972 — p. 38

[3] Roosevelt, *The Autobiography of Eleanor Roosevelt,* 1992 — p. 305

[4] Lash J. P., *Eleanor: The Years Alone,* 1972 — p. 38

[5] Ibid. p. 48

[6] Ibid. p. 45

[7] Roosevelt, *The Autobiography of Eleanor Roosevelt,* 1992 — p. 397

[8] Lash J. P., *Eleanor: The Years Alone,* 1972 — p. 70

[9] Ibid. p. 106

[10] Ibid. p. 69

[11] Ibid. p. 106

[12] Roosevelt, *The Autobiography of Eleanor Roosevelt,* 1992 — p. 320

[13] Ibid. p. 308

[14] Lash J. P., *Eleanor: The Years Alone,* 1972 — p. 56

[15] Ibid. p. 239

[16] Cook, *Eleanor Roosevelt, Volume 2, The Defining Years, 1933 - 1938,* 1999 — p. 440

Chapter Fourteen — Elanor

[1] Lash J. P., *Eleanor: The Years Alone,* 1972 — p. 191

[2] Ibid. p. 192

[3] Ibid. p. 190

[4] Ibid. p. 199

[5] Roosevelt, *My Day, the Best of Eleanor Roosevelt's Acclaimed Newspaper Columns,* 1936-1962, 2001 — p. 183

[6] Ibid. p. 251

[7] Lash J. P., *Eleanor: The Years Alone,* 1972 — p. 200

[8] Ibid. p. 156

[9] Goodwin, 1994 — p. 205

[10] Roosevelt, *You Learn By Living,* 1960 — p. 157

[11] Lash J. P., *Eleanor: The Years Alone,* 1972 — p. 338-339

[12] Ibid. p. 302

[13] Lash J. P., *Eleanor and Franklin,* 1971 — p. 378

[14] Lash J. P., *Eleanor: The Years Alone,* 1972 — p. 239

[15] Cook, *Eleanor Roosevelt, Volume 2, The Defining Years, 1933 - 1938,* 1999 — p. 94

[16] Lash J. P., *Eleanor: The Years Alone*, 1972 — p. 182

[17] Roosevelt, *You Learn By Living*, 1960 — p. 96

[18] Roosevelt, *The Autobiography of Eleanor Roosevelt*, 1992 — p. 412

[19] Lash J. P., *Eleanor: The Years Alone*, 1972 — p. 323

[20] Ibid. p. 330

INDEX

A

Adams, Clover, 42, 43, 44, 45
Adams, Henry, 41,42,43,44
Adams, John (President), 41
Adams, John Quincy
  (President), 41
African Americans, (see also
  Negroes), 57. 58, 149
Allenswood, 10, 13, 2
Anderson, Marian, 74, 75
Anti-lynching, 67, 71, 72,
Anti-Semitism, 81, 83, 126
Army, 77, 90
Arthurdale project, 62, 63
Associated Press, 51
Astor, 5, 6, 109

B

Baruch, Bernard, 81
Bethune, Mary McLeod, 66,
  77

C

Campobello, 23, 27, 32, 33,
  46, 48, 65, 110
Chazy Lake, 49
Child labor, 135
Churchill, Clementine, 106,
  107
Churchill, Winston, 106, 107,
  116, 149
Civilian Conservation Corps
  (CCC), 56, 60

Civil rights movement, 125,
  139
Communism, 99, 100, 105
Comission of Human Rights
  137, 140
Connor, Eugene "Bull", 73
Cook, Nancy, 48, 111, 113,
  115, 116

D

Daughters of the American
  Revolution (DAR), 74, 75,
  130
Declaration of Human
  Rights, see Universal
  Declaration of Human
  Rights
Democratic Convention
  1932, 50
Depression, The Great, 54,
  56, 60, 62, 80, 113
Dickerman, Marion, 111, 113,
  116, 115
Du Bois, W.E.B., 139
Dulles, John Foster, 104, 140

E

Earhart, Amelia, 52, 109
  education, 12, 13, 70
Einstein, Albert, 147
Eisenhower, Dwight D. 103

F

Federal Bureau of Investi-

gation (FBI), 104, 145
France, 32, 88

G

Germany, Stuttgart, 132

H

Hall, Grandmother or Mrs., 9, 10, 11, 12, 13, 14, 15, 16, 17, 18, 55, 79
Hall, see Roosevelt Gracie Hall (Eleanor's brother), 9, 11, 12, 17, 49, 115, 116
Halsey, Admiral, 90, 91
Heart, William Randolph, 129
Hickock, Lorena (Hick), 51, 54, 109, 110, 112, 147
Hitler, Adolf 72, 81, 88, 89
Hyde Park, N.Y. 29, 111

I

India, 5, 145
Italy, 15, 135

J

Japan, 76, 135
Jews, 20, 50, 64, 67, 81, 82, 83, 85, 126, 132, 140, 146

K

Kennedy, John F., 116, 148, 149
Khrushchev, Nikita, 133, 145

L

League of Nations, 134, 135
League of Women Voters, 145

Longworth, Alice Roosevelt – see Roosevelt, Alice
Lynching, 64, 65, 66, 71,72

M

Marion, see Dickerman, Marion
McCall's, 47
McCarthy, Joe (Senator), 99, 100, 103, 104
Mercer, Lucy, 32, 33, 34, 43, 117, 118, 119
Meir, Golda, 126, 127, 149, 151
Miller, Earl, 114, 115
"My Day" (Eleanor's column), 28, 54, 72, 91, 93, 103, 131

N

Nan – see Cook, Nancy
National Association for the Advancement of Colored People (NAACP), 67, 139
National Conference on Fundamental Problems in the Education of Negroes, 70
Navy, 26, 28, 71, 87, 90
Nazi, 72, 88, 93, 131, 132
Neal, Claude, 67, 68, 139
Negroes, 3, 76
Nesbitt, Henrietta, 115
New Deal, 61, 62, 71, 80
New York Herald, 8

New York Metropolitan Opera, 54

New York Times, 52, 106

P

Patton, George, 67, 95

Paul, Alice, 112

Pegler, Westbrook, 104, 136

Psyche, poem, 34, 35

Pussie, Aunt, 15, 17

R

Redbook Magazine, 47

Red Cross, 32, 91

Red Scare, 99

Refugees, 134, 140

Riots, 65, 73, 74, 130

Rock Creek Cemetery, 42, 44, 51

Roosevelt (Longworth), Alice, 33

Roosevelt, Anna (mother), 5, 6, 7, 8, 9

Roosevelt, Anna (daughter), 29, 32, 116, 119, 147

Roosevelt, Betsey Cushing (daughter-in-law), 111

Roosevelt, Ellie (Eleanor's brother), 9

Roosevelt, Elliott (father), 5, 6, 7, 8, 9, 10, 15

Roosevelt, Elliott (son), 27, 29, 32, 109, 119, 147

Roosevelt, Franklin Delano (husband), 19, 20, 21, 22, 23, 34, 25, 26, 27, 28, 31, 32, 33, 34, 42, 34, 42, 44, 45, 46, 47, 48, 49, 50, 51, 54, 55, 62, 65, 66, 67, 69, 72, 73, 77, 78, 81, 82, 83, 94, 101, 102, 108, 110. 111, 112, 113, 114, 115, 116, 118, 119, 120, 129, 130, 132, 146, 150,

Roosevelt, Franklin Delano, Jr. (son), 32, 108, 109, 147

Roosevelt, Gracie Hall (brother), 9, 11, 12, 17, 49, 115, 116

Roosevelt, James (Franklin's father) 21

Roosevelt, James (son), 32, 111, 114, 147

Roosevelt, John (son), 32, 147

Roosevelt, Sara Delano (mother-in-law), 20, 21, 22, 23, 24, 25, 26, 27, 28, 45, 46, 47, 66, 81, 101, 108, 109, 110, 111, 114, 147

Roosevelt, Theodore, Jr. (uncle and president), 5, 8, Uncle Teddy, 10, 18, 25, 125, 126

S

Shapiro, Feige, 56

Social security, 60, 61

Southern Conference on Human Welfare (SCHW), 73

Souvestre, Mlle. Marie, 14, 15, 16, 17, 36
Soviet Union, 138, 140
Strike, 48

T

Thompson, Malvina (Tommy), 53, 113
Todhunter School, 47
Truman, Harry S, 117, 118, 132, 134, 149

U

Unemployment, 4, 47
Unemployment insurance, 47
United Nations, 134, 135, 136, 137, 139, 140, 141, 142
Universal Declaration of Human Rights, 135, 137, 141, 142, 143, 151

V

Val-Kill, 72, 110, 111, 113, 116, 121, 122, 149, 150
Vanderbilts, 5, 21
Veterans, 3, 65, 87, 99
Vishinsky, Andrei, 138, 141

W

Warm Springs, Georgia, 73, 77, 111, 117, 118
White, Walter, 67, 139
White House, 51, 52, 55, 56, 74, 77, 79, 106, 112, 115, 117, 119, 121, 136
Wilson, Woodrow, 78

Women's Trade Union League, 47, 56
World Court, 128, 129, 130
World Foundation, 128
World Health Organization, 134, 135
World War I or WWI, 31, 32, 65, 87, 88, 93, 128, 129, 134, 149
World War II or WWII, 83, 84, 87, 88, 99, 117, 129, 130, 131, 132, 135, 140
World Women's Party for Equal Rights, 138

Y

Yosemite National Park, 51, 110

Z

Zionism, 83, 126

Additional copies of *Eleanor Roosevelt's Life of
Soul Searching and Self Discovery*
are available through your favorite
book dealer or from the publisher:

Flash History Press
P.O. Box 184
Paoli, PA 19301
Website: www.AnnAtkins.com

Eleanor Roosevelt's Life
(ISBN: 978-0-9834784-0-9)
is $19.95 for softbound edition
plus sales tax for PA orders.
Includes
Free Shipping and Handling
and $1.00 donation to charity
(Ann will match the $1.00 donation).

Charities will include:
Ronald McDonald House
Shelters for Abused Women and Children
Eddie's House (for aged out Foster children)
Habitat for Humanity